HEARING
GOD'S VOICE
MADE SIMPLE

HEARING GOD'S VOICE
MADE SIMPLE

Praying Medic

INKITY
PRESS™

Inkity Press™
137 East Elliot Road, #2292, Gilbert, AZ 85234

This book and other Inkity Press titles can be found at:
InkityPress.com and PrayingMedic.com

Available from Amazon.com, CreateSpace.com, and other retail outlets.

For more information visit our website at **www.inkitypress.com**
or email us at **admin@inkitypress.com** or **admin@prayingmedic.com**

ISBN-13: 978-0692586389 (Inkity Press)
ISBN-10: 0692586385

Printed in the U.S.A.

THIS BOOK IS DEDICATED TO my niece and my editor, Lydia Blain, whom I'm also pleased to call my friend. It is a joy to be able to work with a woman of such talent and wit, and to watch her grow in her relationship with God.

··························
ACKNOWLEDGMENTS

IT IS MY PLEASURE TO thank the many people who have helped in the development of this book by contributing to my public discussions and by leaving comments on the articles I've posted. You know who you are. I greatly value your experiences, your insights and your encouragement.

In addition, I want to specifically thank my friends Jeremy Mangerchine, Jesse Birkey, Michael VanVlymen and Matthew Robert Payne for their support of the concept of this book. Thanks also go out to Matt Evans, Steve Harmon and Michael King for their friendship and for their willingness to provide feedback on my revelation and experiences. I'd also like to thank David McLain and Todd Adams; I'm so grateful for their daily love and encouragement in my life and work.

I'd like to thank Lydia Blain, my editor, who worked so patiently with me on this book. When I sent her the manuscript, this was *not* the book I had intended to write. There is only so much improvement a writer can make with a manuscript on their own. After that, any improvement must come with the help of someone else. I knew once the manuscript was in Lydia's hands, it would start to become the book I really wanted to write. A good editor knows how to bring the best out of a writer and thanks to her work, this book was transformed into the one I originally intended to write.

I'd like to thank my wife who has as much time and energy invested in this book as I have. She wears many hats in the process of helping me birth my book ideas. Her work on the first round of raw content editing of this manuscript has been invaluable, and her skill in creating interior page layouts and cover designs never ceases to amaze me. Thanks baby, you're the best!

INTRODUCTION

MANY OF US ARE IN need of a new and better understanding of God. I suspect even more that most of us desperately need a new understanding of ourselves. I won't pretend this book isn't what it is—an attempt to change your mind about who God is and who you are. Whether you are an agnostic, a leader in the church, or a believer who is simply interested in learning to hear God a little more clearly, this book was written for you.

If you consider yourself to be an atheist or agnostic, take heart in knowing that not long ago, I shared your views about God. I am not antagonistic toward them. I respect them and I'll do everything I can to validate them, but I will attempt to show you why I no longer share your views.

If you're a Christian, whether a seasoned saint or a new believer, this book is intended to train and equip you. If you're not certain that you're hearing from God, or if you'd simply like to improve your ability to hear what He says, this book provides instruction and exercises you can do to increase your sensitivity to His voice.

If you're a leader in the church, this book can help you better handle your leadership responsibilities. One difficulty with being a leader is the sense of overwhelm that comes from feeling that we have a responsibility to hear God for others. The burden can be oppressive at times. But this burden can be lessened by teaching people to hear God for themselves. One of the objectives of this book is to show you how to help others hear the voice of God.

I lived as an atheist for most of my life. I was comfortable with the belief that God did not exist and *could* not exist because of the horror I saw all around me. I could not imagine a God who called Himself good, putting His stamp of approval on the senseless violence, pain, and tragedy that existed under His rule. If God were all powerful and able to prevent these things from happening, why didn't He? If He could not prevent them, He could not be an all powerful God. I reasoned that if He could prevent them and didn't, He must surely be an insane deity who is unworthy of my tears, much less my adoration or worship.

God managed to convince me that He did in fact exist and that the terms of His existence made violence and pain unavoidable, at least for now. He showed me how He is actively opposing violence in ways I never imagined. And He revealed a few things I didn't expect. One was that He is a heavenly Father with a sense of humor to match my own. I found Him to be a person full of wisdom and power, but also the gentlest of souls. Even more to my surprise was the fact that He seemed to like me. I have relatives who can barely stand to be around me for a weekend, but the Father I met seemed genuinely obsessed with being in my company. Despite the many things I had done wrong, He had the audacity to tell me that I was the apple of His eye. These are but a few of the things I've learned from God after I began listening to Him.

Although the main subject of this book is the person of God, He can at times be best understood through the experiences we have in His kingdom. In order to help reveal that kingdom, I've created a series of books where I illustrate God's kingdom in different ways. All the books in the series *The Kingdom of God Made Simple* are intended to reveal aspects of His kingdom that lie hidden, but which are being revealed to us as we seek them. I say "we" because I don't write exclusively from my own experiences. I'm very active on social media and I've made a habit of asking discussion questions where I elicit the experiences and observations of friends who allow me to publish them. I also interview people about the experiences they've had in the kingdom, and some of what they share finds its way into my books. My desire is to give readers the broadest possible view of God's kingdom as it is being revealed to His people.

Because the views and experiences of my friends are quite diverse, I've frequently found my beliefs being challenged. I once preferred having a neat and tidy view of God. It made life easier, even if it was less exciting and adventurous. I once read books more with an eye to find error than to discover truth. I had my theology all worked out and I looked for anything that didn't square with my beliefs. The fruit of that way of viewing God was a lack of spiritual growth. There is nothing that hinders spiritual growth more than doubt and skepticism. My resistance to anything that seemed novel or strange prevented me from wandering anywhere off the well-worn path that had been traveled by those who had gone before me. Little did I know that God wanted to meet me far from that path.

There is a passage in the book *Alice in Wonderland* that illustrates a point I'd like to consider. Upon coming to a fork in the road she was traveling, Alice asked the Cheshire Cat "Would you tell me, please, which way I ought to go from here?"

"That depends a good deal on where you want to get to," said the Cat.

"I don't much care where," said Alice.

"Then it doesn't matter which way you go," said the Cat.

It's my hope that you're reading this book because you're interested in learning about the kingdom of God. Some of you have found the kingdom while others are still looking for it. Some years ago, almost by accident, I found the path that leads to the kingdom. There are other paths you might choose to follow, but they all lead to other places. If you don't care where you end up, any path will take you there. But there is only one path that leads to the kingdom of God. There is also a gate through which you must go if you want to enter that kingdom.

There are other gates you may choose to enter, but they too, lead to other places. Jesus is the only gate to the kingdom of God.

Contrary to what many people teach, God's kingdom is not really about "religion." It's about a relationship. We enter God's kingdom by entering into a relationship with Him, through Jesus. I didn't like this proposition when I first heard it. We don't like being told there is only one way to do something. But I found that when I accepted Jesus' offer of friendship, I received much more than I expected.

Once I was inside the gate, I realized that the narrow path I took to get there disappeared and before me I saw a spiritual kingdom of limitless possibilities. Those possibilities are revealed to us as we learn to communicate with God. This book is designed to help you hear Him more accurately so you can fully understand who He is and what it means to be one of His children.

I would ask one favor of you. As you read, come with an open mind and an open heart. If you come inclined to find error, or with a heart full of skepticism, you will likely gain nothing from this book, and I want you to profit from your reading. The kingdom of God can only be received by those who seek it with the simplicity and wonder of a child. Skepticism and unbelief prevent the kingdom from being revealed and from having it bear fruit in our lives. I will do my best to present the realities of the kingdom in the simplest terms that I can.

Some of what you'll read may challenge your current beliefs. When such challenges occur, rather than reject them out of hand, you might consider them prayerfully. Aristotle said, "It is the mark of an educated mind to be able to entertain a thought without accepting it." I won't ask you to accept anything in this book simply because I wrote it. All I ask is that when an objectionable idea confronts you, that you consider it prayerfully.

I've often heard people say they don't believe they are hearing from God. I once said the same thing myself. There are those who seem to hear from God with no trouble at all. When we see these people receiving revelation that is obviously from God, it's easy to think they have something we don't. I'm going to let you in on a little secret. Most of us are hearing from God all the time and we don't know it. Looking back, I now see that even as an atheist, God was speaking to me, though at the time, I reasoned it away as something else.

The most common reaction I heard from readers of my previous book *Seeing in the Spirit Made Simple* was the sudden realization that they had been seeing visions from God for quite some time, but were not aware of it. In the same way that we often see visions from God without knowing it, we are all hearing His voice right now. Many of us simply have difficulty picking out His voice from the noise we're being bombarded with. The goal of this book is to help you realize that God is already speaking to you in a variety of ways. Our focus will be to help you develop your ability to recognize the many ways in which He is speaking so that you can discern what He is saying.

Thank you for joining me on this journey.

~ Praying Medic

PART ONE
Is God Speaking?

My Testimony

I WASN'T ALWAYS AWARE THAT God was speaking to me. As a child I was raised in the Catholic Church, but at the age of 12, I became dissatisfied with what I perceived to be religious hypocrisy in those who attended church. I told my parents I wanted nothing more to do with their religion and stopped attending mass on Sunday. In high school and particularly in college, I learned about evolution and soon became a hardened atheist. For most of my adult life I lived in complete indifference to God. I never wondered if He existed, much less whether I had ever heard Him speak. I was fairly certain He had not spoken to me and I was convinced that the people who thought they had heard Him were hearing something they only *thought* was God. Like so many atheists, I hated born again Christians whom I saw as weak-minded people. I especially mistrusted anyone who claimed to hear God's voice. All of that changed on May 25th, 2000, when God finally got my attention.

During this time, I was working as a paramedic-firefighter, or in my case, what we refer to in the business as a para-god. I'd reached a place in my career where I was so full of pride that I wouldn't take correction from my paramedic partner. I had some wrong attitudes toward our patients and the care we gave them. My partner tried to correct me, but I wouldn't hear it. He was younger and less experienced than me. But deep inside, I knew he was right. I was making some bad decisions. I just didn't want to admit it. We had many heated arguments over the course of several months. It became obvious that there was no hope of ever reconciling with him unless I waved the white flag of surrender and stopped playing games. My will to keep up the charade was gone. I just wanted peace. So I told him I was sorry for all the things I'd put him through. I told him he was right and I was wrong. And through a river of tears, I told him I was sorry for destroying our friendship.

After my partner and I buried the hatchet, the stressful work environment cooled off and things went back to normal. A couple of weeks later, he told me about a book he was reading. It was a fictional book that discussed events that were happening in the world and he thought I might like it. I told him I wasn't a fan of fiction, but that I might check it out. I asked what the name of the book was. He said it was called *Left Behind*.

A few weeks after this, because I wanted to earn a little extra money, I signed up to work a 48-hour shift on the Saturday and Sunday of Memorial Day weekend. Memorial Day is one of the busiest weekends of the year, and I felt like I might regret the decision when it was over. Who really wants to spend 48 hours getting brutalized by going on one call after another with no chance of rest? On the Thursday before Memorial Day, my lieutenant and I got into a conversation about a book he was reading. He said it was a great book and he thought I would find it fascinating. The name of the book was *Left Behind*.

I thought it strange that two people would recommend the same book to me a few weeks apart. My lieutenant said I could borrow the book if I wanted. I declined his offer and didn't think about it again until the next day. I thought maybe I should bring something to read in case it was a slow weekend, even though Memorial Day weekend is never slow. I called my lieutenant and told him I wanted to pick up the book.

I drove to his house and he handed it over with a smile. I tossed it on the passenger seat of my car and drove home.

I went to work the next day, expecting a busy shift. By mid-afternoon we had not run a single call. I was bored, so I went to my car and got the book. I went upstairs to the medic bedroom. No one else was around, so I got cozy in my bunk and began reading. As I read, I was drawn to one character in particular—a middle-aged pilot named Rayford Steele.

Steele was a good husband to his Christian wife, but was not a believer himself. Ray was a self-made man, who didn't need to depend on God. He ran his own affairs and didn't feel like religion had anything to offer him. Ray was confident that if there were a God and if heaven were real, he would probably make it into heaven. He wasn't a serial killer or a pedophile. He was a good man, for the most part. The way he saw it, the minor things he struggled with, like the occasional crush on a flight attendant, could hardly bar him from entering heaven. As I read about his life, I realized that Ray was a lot like me.

As Ray's story unfolded in the book, I began to realize that I was in the same place he was, spiritually. The book suggested that what granted us access to heaven was not our good deeds, but a relationship with Jesus. I knew with certainty that if my connection to Jesus was what qualified me to get into heaven, I was never going to get in. I hated Jesus and despised His followers. I had a hard time even saying His name without feeling disgust and loathing. I had no need for religion or religious bigots and I certainly didn't want to become one. Yet I knew that if Jesus was my ticket to heaven, I was bound to spend eternity in hell.

As I read, I encountered the message of God's love displayed in the death of Jesus. This wasn't a new concept to me. I'd known about His death and his resurrection since I was a boy. But I never thought He died for *me*. I understood that His death was a factual event, but it never meant anything to me personally, until this moment. Tears welled up in my eyes as I thought about him suffering and dying for me.

For me? Why did God care about me? What did I ever do to deserve anything from Him? I was just another guy trying to live my own life and stay out of trouble. Why did God care about me?

As I lay in bed thinking about eternity, I sensed that I wasn't alone. There was someone in the room with me. I began having a conversation in my mind with someone who seemed to know everything about me. I'm a good person, I thought. Why do I need Jesus?

Suddenly, my mind began to recall every selfish thing I'd ever done and every mean thing I'd ever said. The presence that was with me began to challenge me. "Are you really a good person? What about all these terrible things you've done?"

Although I didn't believe in God, I suspected that the mysterious presence in the room with me was Him. There was no way to hide my past from this being. The only one who could know such things would be God. Thinking about the selfish things I'd done, how could I call myself a good person? I wasn't a murderer, but I certainly wasn't a saint.

I closed my eyes and tried to block out the thoughts He was bringing to my remembrance. I wept for hours, wrestling on the one hand with fear of spending eternity in hell, and on the other with giving in to a God I've never known. My mind was bombarded with thoughts; what would people think if I became one of those religious hypocrites?

I didn't want to be a believer. I tried desperately to fight the feelings of surrender, but I was losing the battle. It was as if I were dangling in the atmosphere between heaven and earth. I clung desperately to the life that I had, but I was losing my grip. I had to make a decision. I knew that if I let go of my life, I would drop into an unknown abyss that lay beyond my comprehension. But if I clung to my present life, I would spend eternity in darkness.

It was late in the evening when I finally surrendered. Feeling broken and desperate, I said, "God... I don't believe in you. But I give up. I'm tired of living for myself. My life is a mess and I can't fix it. I don't know how to change it. I can't do it myself. If you want me to change, you need to give me a voice or something to follow." After saying these words, I fell asleep on a pillow soaked with tears.

I awoke in the morning to the awareness that something was different. As I lie in bed, I heard a mysterious voice, softly speaking in a way that brought peace to my mind. It was not an external voice, but an internal one. Internal, and yet... not mine.

It's difficult to describe what it's like to someone who hasn't experienced it. There was a soft, whispering voice blowing gently through my soul. It wasn't my own mind. They weren't my own thoughts. They belonged to someone else. The thoughts were distinct and different from the type of thoughts I would think. There was a quality to the voice that was unlike anything I'd ever heard. It was soothing to my soul. Then suddenly, I remembered what happened the night before. I asked God to give me a voice to follow and this voice seemed to be exactly that.

I went downstairs to the day room and met a firefighter. I was about to say something to him, but the voice gently reminded me to be kind. When I met another firefighter, the voice reminded me to say something nice instead of something sarcastic. With each person I met, the voice gave me direction. "Be nice." "Be kind." "Don't be grumpy."

What was going on? I wondered. Who was this voice and how long would it be with me?

Eventually I came to realize that the Spirit of God had come to live inside of me. There was no other plausible explanation. The voice I heard was the voice of God. The Jesus I had always hated was living inside me and had come to be my friend. The Christians I had always despised were now my family. I went to bed an atheist and awoke in the morning a born again Christian. Although this can be a gradual, barely perceptible experience for some, mine was a dramatic, overnight transformation.

CHAPTER TWO

My Sheep Hear My Voice

THERE IS MUCH DEBATE OVER whether God is speaking to us today. After I became a believer, I attended a church that taught from the fundamentalist perspective. Fundamentalism places the highest authority on the scriptures. It teaches that the Bible is the inspired, inerrant, and authoritative word of God. There's nothing wrong with this idea, but fundamentalism also teaches that the Bible is the *final* word from God to man. It says there is no more revelation that we can receive from God, except what has already been given to us in the Bible. In essence, Fundamentalism states that God spoke through the prophets and the apostles who recorded the revelation they received in the scriptures, and since then, He has had nothing more to say to us.

After years of attending a Fundamentalist church I began attending a Charismatic one. One difference between Charismatics and Fundamentalists is that Charismatics believe God is still speaking today. One day a woman came to our church and prophesied to the congregation. She went from one person to another giving them words of encouragement that seemed to represent God's desire for their lives. Somehow, she was able to hear God's thoughts about others and she spoke what she heard. She was not a member of the congregation and didn't know any of the people she prophesied to. She lived in another state. She was in town for a brief period to host a workshop. The words she spoke were accurate. I knew many of these people and I knew what she said was true.

It became apparent to me that day that God is still speaking to us. This woman was clearly hearing from Him for other people. And I had to assume that if she was hearing from God, the rest of us could, too. Since then I've learned that He is speaking to us in a many ways, some of which I had never imagined.

Jesus said to His disciples:

> *"But he who enters by the door is the shepherd of the sheep. To him the doorkeeper opens, and the sheep hear his voice; and he calls his own sheep by name and leads them out. And when he brings out his own sheep, he goes before them; and the sheep follow him, for they know his voice. Yet they will by no means follow a stranger, but will flee from him, for they do not know the voice of strangers."*
> JN. 10:2-5

This observation is literally true of sheep. They learn to recognize the voice of their shepherd. Once they know his voice, if another shepherd calls to them, they will not follow him. Jesus used this illustration from nature to explain the relationship He would have with His disciples. He revealed two things which could not be clearer: The first is that He has a voice which we can hear. He did not say His sheep *may* hear His voice, but that they *will* hear His voice, whether they realize it or not.

Imagine you have a neighbor who has a dog that barks loudly whenever a car drives down the street. Imagine that your hearing is perfect and when the dog barks, you hear it. After a few years of hearing the dog bark, you learn to tune out the barking, even to the point that when a friend visits and mentions it, you might realize you had completely forgotten about the barking dog. You still hear the barking, but you've chosen to live as if you didn't hear it. And that is what Jesus is saying in this passage. That try as we might to ignore His voice, or believe that He is not speaking to us, He is speaking in a way that we can hear.

The second point He makes is that there is a stranger who has a voice we can also hear. I would interpret His reference to the "stranger" as the voice of Satan or demonic beings. The stranger has a voice we can hear. He did not say His sheep would not *hear* the voice of a stranger, but that when they did hear it, they would discern that it was not the voice they should follow. When they heard it, they would flee because they're able to discern which voice is speaking and which they should follow.

This is at the crux of the debate over whether God is still speaking to us today. Fundamentalists fear that if God and demons were both speaking, we would not be able to tell which one was speaking and we'd be led astray. They prefer to settle the question by believing God is not speaking. They believe this view takes all risk out of the equation and provides a safer alternative.

The Bible is clear about the existence of angels and demons. If they exist, it's because there is a purpose for their existence. Angels, demons, God, and Satan are all real and they speak to us every day in their own spiritual language. Demons assist in the work of the kingdom of darkness and angels assist in the work of the kingdom of heaven.

It does no good for us to put our heads in the sand and pretend they don't exist and are not speaking to us. What we must do is learn how to discern one from the other so that we can receive revelation from God and reject revelation that is not from Him. Becoming a fully mature believer requires us to discern life from death, truth from error, and the kingdom of God from the kingdom of darkness. If we never learn to distinguish one voice from another, we cannot grow into fully mature children of God.

CHAPTER THREE

Misconceptions and Myths

THIS CHAPTER IS PROVIDED FOR the benefit of those who are not certain that God is speaking to us today, or who are concerned that we may be led astray if we try to hear His voice. If you have such concerns, it's my hope that this chapter will answer your concerns and clear up any misconceptions you may have. I've provided a number of common objections people have to hearing God's voice in bold, and my responses, which follow them.

"God does not speak directly to man."

There are many people both inside and outside the church who do not believe God is speaking directly to us. Those outside the church have dismissed claims from those who said they have heard God speak because many of these people have committed crimes and atrocities that God allegedly told them to commit. We seem to instinctively know that if God were to exist and if He were to speak to us, He would not endorse such violent behavior. This is, by the way, one of the main reasons why many atheists dismiss the God that Christians preach. When an atheist hears of a God who seems to endorse mass genocide and other acts of cruelty and violence, their internal understanding (that if God existed, He would be more loving than this) causes them to reject the violent and immoral God who is preached from many pulpits. When atheists and agnostics are presented with the idea that God is a truly loving and compassionate deity, many will confess that they hope such a God does exist.

While those inside the church agree that salvation comes by having a personal relationship with God through Jesus, many do not believe that this relationship includes having a direct dialogue with God. Their view is that we can speak to God through prayer, but He speaks back to us through the scriptures, and perhaps through the circumstances of our lives, but not through direct, personal revelation. The main reason for this view is the fear that if God were to speak to us directly, we might be inclined to value the Bible less and value our conversations with God more, perhaps even to the point of disregarding the Bible completely and living only by what we hear from God.

If we teach that salvation is having a relationship with God through the indwelling of the Holy Spirit, but that the Holy Spirit does not communicate directly with us, then we might ask a few questions:

Are we to believe that this "relationship" does not involve communication between two parties? And if God does not speak to us directly, then how does He correct, encourage, and console us?

While it's true that some people find encouragement and consolation by reading the scriptures, how do we imagine that God did these things before the scriptures were written, and how does He do them today for people who do not have Bibles, or are unable to read them?

Are we to believe that the Bible is the only way in which God speaks to man? Some teach that God only speaks to us through the Bible, which brings us to our next objection.

"God speaks to us through the Bible. We don't need anything more."

God does without question speak to us through the Bible. The scriptures have been given to us for correction, for doctrine, for instruction in righteousness, and for encouragement. The Bible is indispensable as a guide that points us to God. But a person who reads the Bible can fall into error if their study is not guided by the voice of God.

I once listened to a group of pastors who were part of a popular non -denominational assembly of churches. They were solid Bible teachers, but they had allowed what I would consider a few false doctrines into their theology, one of them was the idea that healing and miracles had ceased thousands of years ago. I once believed what they taught. Being good Bible teachers, they had their handful of Bible verses to back up their teaching. Although they meant no harm, they had nonetheless embraced some false teachings along the way and they were teaching them to their congregations.

The truth of the matter came to me one day, not as I studied the Bible, but in a dream where God Himself told me He wanted me to pray for my patients to be healed. I didn't believe in healing at the time, but flatly rejected it. I didn't accept healing mostly because these Bible teachers had persuaded me not to. They believed healing was not happening today, and I believed what they taught. I had to change my thinking and begin reading the Bible with a new set of eyes. When I did, I saw the many accounts of healing and the clear instructions Jesus gave to His disciples to heal the sick. I realized that supernatural healing is one of the most irrefutable doctrines of the New Testament, despite the fact that many good Bible teachers refuse to see it as such. Here's a case where personal revelation from God was needed to straighten out a lie I had learned from some of the best Bible teachers in the world.

There is no guarantee that a strict diet of scripture reading will lead us along the complete path of truth. If you read without having the Holy Spirit teach your spirit and interpret the scriptures for you, the exercise may very well lead you to a warped understanding of God. All the major pseudo-Christian cults teach from the Bible. Their error is in not having the Spirit of God interpret and apply what they read.

DON'T AGREE

✗

"God speaks to us through leaders and not personally."

After I became a believer, I began attending church, reading the Bible, and listening to audio sermons. As I studied the Bible, the things I encountered challenged everything I believed. The Spirit of God made impressions in my mind testifying that what I had read was true. It was a time of having my mind established in the foundational truths of Christianity. As time went on, I found myself relying more on sermons from Bible teachers than on direct revelation from the Holy Spirit. During this time, I seldom heard the voice of God clearly for myself. Most of what I referred to as "hearing from God" came through messages from church leaders. But the day finally came when God wanted to teach me things that men couldn't, and show me things these teachers didn't have a grid for. I needed to learn from a different teacher. I needed to start hearing from God again, personally. So I broke away from the teaching I had grown accustomed to and got myself under the direct instruction of the Holy Spirit again and it's been an amazing journey ever since.

Today, I don't have anyone in my life that I would call my pastor, although I have many people whom I would call mentors. These men and women are my spiritual peer group. We see each other as friends and equals. There is no structure of hierarchy among us. We all receive encouragement, instruction, and occasionally correction from others in the group (if and when we ask for it). We tend to receive most of our instruction directly from God. I still listen to audio messages once in a while and I occasionally attend conferences. I also receive instruction from reading a good book now and then. But these sources of infor-mation are not where I get most of the direction for my personal life. They serve more as confirmation of the things God tells me personally. And none of the people I learn from have earned the right to tell me what's best for me. That responsibility belongs solely to God.

I'm not suggesting that having a pastor is a bad thing. I think we all need someone trustworthy to help us, especially when we're spiritually immature. I'm only relating how God needed me to stop relying mostly on teaching from men so that I could come under His direct instruction. After we've matured as believers, there comes a time when we need to lean more on God for instruction than we do His kids. Jesus is my overseer, my covering, my big brother, and the Shepherd of my soul.

And the Holy Spirit is my schoolmaster. The apostle Paul shared his own story of how he did not go to Jerusalem to be taught by the other apostles after his conversion, but instead he went to Arabia and was instructed by the Lord, personally (see Galatians chapter 1).

It's easy to become dependent on men and women we respect to teach us about God. It's probably easier for most of us to listen to a podcast or video than it is to spend an hour in silence allowing God to speak to our spirit. I don't mind sharing with you what the Holy Spirit teaches me, but I would advise you not to become too dependent on me or anyone else as your main source of instruction. At God's request, I made myself dependent on Him, and that ended my dependence on man. He honored my willingness to come to Him directly and He's made it fairly easy for me to hear Him. Had I chosen to continue relying on men, I probably would not be hearing from Him as easily as I do today. (By "easy" I don't mean that I hear an audible voice speaking to me. I hear Him mostly through barely perceptible thought impressions, like most people. It's just that after a while, discerning His voice isn't as difficult as it can be at the beginning.)

If you're content to hear from men, God will allow you to be instructed by them. But if your heart's desire is to be instructed by God, He will draw you near and teach you Himself, like any good father would. Part of the dynamic of hearing God's voice clearly is deciding in your heart that you want to hear from Him more than you want to hear from others. It's not always easy to make this kind of change, but if God is calling you to do it, I would advise you to pursue it wholeheartedly. You won't regret it.

"When God speaks He will never contradict what is written in the scriptures."

A common teaching today is that God will never contradict anything in the scriptures. The Bible recounts the story of the day when the apostle Peter was praying on a rooftop and he fell into a trance. While in the trance, the Holy Spirit showed him a number of unclean animals and said, "Get up, Peter; kill and eat them." (Acts 10:12 NLT)

The 11th chapter of Leviticus outlines God's instructions to the nation of Israel about which animals they could keep as livestock and eat as food and which they could not. The animals they could keep were called "clean." Those they could not were called "unclean." The Spirit of God had instructed Peter to kill and eat animals that had been designated "unclean."

Peter's response to the Spirit of God was "No, Lord. I have never eaten anything that our Jewish laws have declared impure and unclean." (Acts 10:14 NLT) Peter's position was this: If the Spirit of God were going to speak to him and tell him to do something, it could never contradict what was written in the scriptures. And this was a clear contradiction of what He had instructed them to do. So Peter rejected the Lord's direction. But the Holy Spirit continued saying, "Do not call something unclean if God has made it clean." (Acts 10:15 NLT)

God wanted to give Peter new revelation that he needed to understand, so He showed him the same scene three times. Peter was perplexed by all of this and as he pondered what it meant, three men came looking for him. The Holy Spirit then told Peter "Get up, go downstairs, and go with them without hesitation. Don't worry, for I have sent them." (Acts 10:20 NLT) He had the men stay the night and the next day he went with them to Caesarea, where he visited the house of a Gentile named Cornelius.

When he arrived at the house of Cornelius, Peter confessed that he was still confused, but explained that he was doing his best to follow God's lead: "You know it is against our laws for a Jewish man to enter a Gentile home like this, or to associate with you. But God has shown me that I should no longer think of anyone as impure or unclean." (Acts 10:28 NLT) Peter made the connection between the unclean animals he saw in the trance and the "unclean" Gentiles he was sent to speak with. He bore witness to the miracles, the death, and the resurrection of Jesus before the friends and relatives of Cornelius. They were all saved and baptized and the first Gentiles were added to the church.

The scriptures indicated that certain animals were considered unclean, but at a later date the Lord declared the same animals clean. If Peter would not have been willing to listen to the Holy Spirit, he would never have come to the understanding he needed—that God had now declared that all animals, and more importantly, all people, were now "clean." The fact that the gospel was not only for the Jews, but also for the Gentiles, was a radical deviation from what the disciples had previously understood from the scriptures.

Peter and the leaders of the early church had to wrestle with many new revelations from God that contradicted the plain teaching of scripture. Perhaps no one had more difficulty with this than the Apostle Paul. The early church leaders were familiar with the scriptures, but Paul had been trained as a Pharisee. No one knew the scriptures better than the members of this sect. When the new covenant came, the Holy Spirit gave the apostles a different revelation from what they had known. Much of the new revelation they received from God seemed to plainly disregard what had been written by Moses and the prophets. Paul had many heated debates over the value of circumcision and the various dietary and ceremonial laws he'd been taught to observe. He had previously taught that righteousness came by *keeping* the law, but he would now champion the message that righteousness was found *apart* from the law.

From these events, it seems evident that God does give revelation, albeit rarely, which seems to flatly contradict the scriptures. So where does this leave us?

yes

The scriptures will always be the plumb line by which the doctrines of our faith are measured. We must hold fast to truths that they reveal. But they aren't the *only* way in which revelation can be evaluated. If we receive revelation that seems to contradict scripture or if we can find no reference to it in the Bible, we may need to use a different strategy. Another way to verify the origin of revelation is sharing it with mature believers to see if it rings true with them. This was one of the ways in which early church leaders developed new doctrines. They met and discussed the new revelation they had received and if a new teaching seemed good to them, it was accepted as part of the new covenant teaching. If it did not, it was rejected.

I'm fortunate to travel among a group of very mature believers. We all receive revelation we believe to be from God and some of it can be a little weird. But we trust the others in the group enough to know we can share our latest dream, message, or experience, and receive prayerful and mature discernment about it. Much of what we share is rejected for one reason or another, but some of it has been embraced by the entire group.

"It's too easy to be deceived by voices that are not God's."

It is true that there are many deceiving spirits that would like us to believe they are giving us revelation from God. It's wise to be cautious about which revelation we receive. Some would argue that the safest plan is to stick with what the Bible says and avoid any other revelation. The problem with this idea is that most of us do not read the Bible in a vacuum. We listen to teachers who explain the scriptures to us. Bible teachers do not rely exclusively on the scriptures either. Most of them have attended a Bible college or seminary where they were taught to interpret the Bible by various teachers. These teachers were influenced by other teachers. Anyone who teaches the Bible has been influenced by the collective views of hundreds of people. It's difficult to imagine that none of these people were ever influenced by a deceiving spirit. Mixed in with the truth, there will always be a little error.

Each of us has a unique view of God that is based on books that we've read, teachers we've listened to, views that were held by people who influenced us, and our own personal experiences. Even among those who attend the same church, there are significant differences in the way each person sees God. My closest friends have beliefs about God that I do not agree with. This diversity in our views creates an inconvenient problem I'd like to illustrate:

If I held three coins in my hand and asked you and a friend to guess how many I had, and you guessed two, while your friend guessed five, you would both be wrong. If you guessed three and he guessed four, only you would be right. And if you both guessed three, you would both be right. The point being—there is only one answer that can be correct. Two opposing answers cannot both be correct. At least one of them must be wrong. It's human nature to think that our view of God is true. To think otherwise is to admit that we are deceived.

But because we hold opposing views—all of which cannot be correct—we must admit that we all believe some things about God that are not true. No one has a perfectly accurate view of God. Since we all have some degree of error in our theology, our aim must be to replace our inaccurate beliefs with ones that are closer to the truth.

There is a freedom in admitting that our view of God isn't perfect. It removes the pressure of needing to be right at all cost. When we admit that our view isn't perfect, we have reason to seek a better understanding of who God is. This sets us on a journey of discovery where we're free to explore the beliefs others have and weigh everything by the Spirit. Such freedoms are not everyone's cup of tea. When we allow ourselves this kind of liberty, we do expose ourselves to certain risks.

Receiving revelation directly from God is a risky proposition. There are times when we will think we heard God speak and we'll either misunderstand what was said, or the message will not have come from Him at all. Hearing from God requires us to exercise a measure of faith. Faith is believing and expecting that we will receive what we've asked for—but there is no guarantee of it. Part of the process of maturing as sons and daughters of God is the growth that comes through the process of trial and error.

Some leaders would have us believe that being in error is the unpardonable sin. There is no doubt that as we endeavor to hear from God, we will occasionally hear from a spirit that was not the Spirit of God, and we will be deceived. I believe God's ability to correct us and reveal the truth is greater than the enemy's ability to deceive us. If you do not wish to risk the possibility of being in error, you're free to close this book and find another one to read. But if you're willing to risk being wrong on occasion so that you can truly hear God with accuracy most of the time, you are invited to read on.

CHAPTER FOUR

God Speaks to Everyone

MANY PEOPLE SAY THEY HAVE never heard God speak. If you're convinced that you've never heard Him speak to you, I would suggest that you probably *have* heard Him speak, but not in a way that allowed you to say it was Him without question.

Not long after I became a Christian, I took my family to a water park. We claimed a small piece of real estate beside the pool and spent the day going to and from the water. At the end of the day, I noticed someone had left a camera lying on the ground near where we were sitting. It had been there for several hours and no one seemed to notice it. Most of the people around us were packing up their things to go home and the camera owner was nowhere to be seen. I told my family I was going to turn the camera in to security so they could put it in the lost and found. Someone who heard me said I should keep it. They reasoned that the owner would probably never come back for

39

it. As they were saying this, the voice of God suddenly spoke loudly and more emphatically than I had ever heard before. "NO!" was all He said. But He said this one word so loudly I wondered if those nearby could hear it too. I picked up the camera and took it to the security station.

God has created us in such a way that we can determine the course of our own life without Him interfering with or overriding our decisions. He has given us what is known as *free will*. We are autonomous beings who are free to live however we want according to our plans and desires. Contrary to what is taught by many theologians, God is not in control of the actions of man. Once we decide to do something—whether noble or destructive—God does not interfere. If the leader of a nation decides to kill half the citizens of the nation he rules over, though God may disapprove of his action, He will never directly prevent the leader from committing the evil he has determined to do. Thus, many terrible things take place every day that God does not approve of.

God does have His own plans and desires for each of us. Rather than control us directly like robots, He conveys His will to us through our conscience. He speaks to our soul the things He would like us to know, but in a way that allows us to ignore Him, if we choose. The Bible says that we all have an awareness of His voice through our conscience:

> *"Even Gentiles, who do not have God's written law, show that they know his law when they instinctively obey it, even without having heard it. They demonstrate that God's law is written in their hearts, for their own conscience and thoughts either accuse them or tell them they are doing right."*
> ROM. 2:14-15 NLT

Everyone is able to hear the voice of God through their conscience. When we do right, His voice tells us we've done right. When we do wrong, He tells us we've done wrong. This is one of the ways in which we hear His voice every day. And although some choose to disobey His voice, it's not because they're unable to hear Him. It's because they have heard and they've chosen to ignore Him.

Many people believe they have never heard God's voice because He so seldom tells them what they want to hear. When He speaks contrary to their desires, they ignore Him and pretend He has never spoken. This is how I lived when I was an atheist. I lived the way I wanted to live, sometimes in complete disregard of my conscience. I believed I had never heard God speak, but in fact, He had been speaking to me all along. I simply chose not to listen to Him.

When we habitually ignore our conscience, we become insensitive to what it tells us. His voice grows fainter and we lose our sensitivity and receptivity to it. The apostle Paul illustrated this idea when he said some people have had their conscience seared (see 1 Tim. 4:2). Searing burns the flesh and in doing so kills the nerves, leaving one unable to feel any sensation. By having our conscience seared, we can by the use of our own will become insensitive to hearing God's voice.

If you believe you're not hearing God's voice, one problem might be that you've grown insensitive to it by repeatedly disobeying your conscience. When the Bible says, "If today you hear His voice, harden not your hearts," it is reminding us that we have a choice to make when we hear His voice. We can choose to harden our hearts against Him, or choose to listen and follow Him. If we can become desensitized to His voice, we can also become *more* sensitive to it by exerting our will in agreement with Him. As I illustrated with my own testimony, it's easy to have our conscience made sensitive again. Repentance is a good starting point.

The first message Jesus preached was, "Repent! For the kingdom of Heaven is at hand," (see Mt. 3:2).

The true meaning of "repentance" has become distorted over the years. The word *repent*, which is used in most English Bible translations, comes from the Latin translation of the scriptures. The Latin word from which "repent" is translated implies a change of action in an attempt to gain favor with someone. The earliest texts of the New Testament were not written in Latin, but Greek. The Greek word in this passage has a very different meaning. The Greek word that is translated "repent" is *metanoia*, which comes from two words: *meta*, which refers to a change or transformation; and *noia*, which refers to the mind. The instruction of Jesus was not for people to change their *behavior* to gain favor with God. It was to change their way of *thinking*, because the kingdom of

God had come. The good news is that God is in love with you. The love of God when it is apprehended by the heart of man changes our behavior. When our mind comes into agreement with Him, it becomes easier to hear His voice.

CHAPTER FIVE

Be Still

IN A TYPICAL DAY THERE are a thousand things that scream for our attention. The things that get our attention are the things from which the issues of life flow. As a man thinks in his heart, so he is. The soul of man comes into existence unblemished and uninfluenced, but it leaves this planet with millions of impressions upon it. Every interaction we have with another soul leaves a permanent impression on ours. Every e-mail we receive, every TV show we watch, every hug we give, and every phone call we take changes us in some way. This is why Jesus said that we should, with all diligence, guard our hearts.

In the movie *Truman*, Jim Carrey's character was cast as the star of a television show that took place in a city that was actually a massive television studio where his friends and relatives were all actors. The main character, Truman, didn't know his life was being carefully scripted each week. Occasionally, an outsider would make their way onto the set to warn him that things were not as they seemed. But due to the many distractions provided by the show's cunning producer, the truth about his life eluded him. He was always distracted by someone who got his attention just long enough to keep him from seriously considering the warnings that were being sent.

In a similar way, God is always sending messages to us. If we allow ourselves to become distracted by the people and things that make demands on our time, we may never consider what He is saying, or even hear the messages. For those who are not hearing God as well as they would like to, the problem is that other things have taken the highest priority. Hearing God is mostly a matter of correctly prioritizing the things that have our attention. This is not to say that we can completely ignore our responsibilities and relationships and focus exclusively on God. We need to strike a sensible balance between giving adequate time to thinking about our family, work, and friendships, while setting time aside to focus on what God is saying. As you grow in your ability to hear God's voice, you'll find it easier to do both at the same time.

Jack Nicklaus said golf is a game that you can excel at if you learn how to do a small number of things extremely well, and do them well consistently. I'm not the greatest golfer in the world, but I do know one thing about golf, and it's the fact that if I were to spend ten hours a week on the driving range with a pro who taught me how to properly hit a ball off the tee, I'd be a lot better golfer than I am now. The key to hitting a golf ball consistently is spending hours practicing the little things. It's learning how to keep your head in the right position and not moving it during your swing. It's learning how to hold a club the right way. It's learning how to tune out the distracting things going on around you. It's learning to do the many small things right and doing them consistently so that you always hit the ball the same way.

The process of learning how to hear the voice of God is no different. Learning how to pick out the voice of the Holy Spirit from among the other voices that demand our attention is a process we can learn by doing a few things repeatedly. There are steps we can take to filter out the noise and ways by which we can verify we're hearing God accurately. If we can learn to do these things consistently, we'll have no trouble hearing His voice.

Imagine you and I were to walk into a high school band room filled with students warming up for a performance. We would hear trumpets, trombones, tubas, saxophones, and clarinets practicing scales and playing parts of the performance. When all these sounds are combined, it's difficult to distinguish anything that sounds like a song. Now imagine I ask if you can hear a piccolo playing a song. A piccolo is a high pitched instrument that does not project very well. You would need to listen very closely to pick out a piccolo playing a song from among the other instruments.

You might say you weren't able to hear the piccolo playing a song because there was too much noise. While it may be true that the other instruments will create enough noise to make it difficult to hear the piccolo, the fact remains that the piccolo is still playing a song, even if we don't recognize it. God's voice operates in the same way. Many of us have concluded that because we haven't recognized God's voice, He isn't speaking. But He is speaking to us whether we recognize it or not. If we want to hear Him, we must find a way to reduce the noise that drowns out His voice.

It's easier to focus on hearing God in an environment that is free of distractions. Many people find it helpful to spend time in a secluded, silent location as they focus on hearing His voice. This is not because God speaks more or because He speaks louder in such places, but because it's easier to hear Him when background noises are eliminated. Although He can and does speak to us in virtually any setting, most novices find it helpful to be in a setting that is free of distractions. Once you've practiced, you'll be able to hear His voice in a noisy environment, but it's best to begin in a quiet place.

Meditation

There is much that can be learned about communing and communicating with God by studying the life of the psalmists of the Bible. Despite the fact that they suffered incredible hardship and adversity, it's clear that they found great solace, wisdom, and power in times of quiet meditation. David wrote in Psalm 145 verse 5, *"I will meditate on your majestic, glorious splendor and your wonderful miracles."*

When we speak of Christian meditation, we're not referring to the type of meditation used by eastern religions and New Age practitioners. Some practitioners of meditation try to empty their mind of all thought. Others try to come into harmony with an impersonal force or seek understanding from the universe.

Christians on the other hand, meditate on the person of God, who is a loving Father to us all. Meditation as it was practiced by the psalmists and which has been used by believers throughout the entire church age focuses on our oneness with God. It's tuning out external noise and becoming quiet in our soul so that we might focus on the person of God. When our mind has been cleared of other thoughts, we're able to focus on His goodness, His mercy, or His other characteristics, so that we might receive whatever He wants to impart to us—whether peace, wisdom, healing, or something else. This is what the psalmist meant when he wrote, "Be still and know that I am God."

For those who are not well-acquainted with hearing God's voice, it may be helpful at first, to spend time in a somewhat isolated environment. Something as simple as taking a 20-minute walk, several times a week on a quiet road in the country can be a good way to find time to meditate in silence.

Another strategy might be to spend 20 or 30 minutes at the end of the day before bed time, in a comfortable chair, quietly meditating on God. Meditating on the goodness of God is an excellent way to grow in your ability to hear Him. As we meditate on His goodness, it tends to produce thankfulness and gratitude in us. These attitudes can lead us to praise Him. Psalm 100 says:

Come before His presence with singing.
Enter into His gates with thanksgiving,
And into His courts with praise.
PS. 100:2, 4

Singing, thanksgiving, and praise can serve as gates through which we enter into the presence of God. Meditation is not a goal in itself. It is something like a launching pad that positions us to have an encounter with God.

Exercise

Meditation can seem difficult or strange if you're not familiar with it, but let me assure you, there's less mystery to it than you might think. Forget whatever preconceptions you might have about what it means to meditate. The process of meditation itself can be virtually anything you want it to be. Some people begin meditation by allowing a familiar worship song to invade their mind. As a worship song plays in their mind, other competing thoughts tend to dissipate. That's the main goal of meditation—to displace the mental clutter that occupies our mind, which allows our mind to be filled with the thoughts of God. Meditation can be as simple as turning your thoughts intentionally toward God and turning them *away* from whatever else you habitually think about. A successful meditation session for a beginner might simply be a five-minute exercise of thinking about the good things God has done for them during the past week. If you're able to do this for five minutes at first, try going ten minutes the next time. You should begin to discern thought impressions in your mind that seem foreign to you. These impressions may be from God. You may feel unusual emotions, such as a deep sense of peace or love. You may begin to see images in your mind that are of heavenly things. These images, emotions, and thoughts may be things God wants you to consider. In later chapters we'll take a look at how we can know if they are from God, how to interpret them, and what we might do with them.

Notes

CHAPTER SIX

Faith and Hearing God's Voice

IF WE WANT TO HEAR God's voice we must come to expect that when we turn our attention toward Him, He will turn His attention toward us. One of the most difficult lessons of learning to hear His voice is getting past the bias we have that makes us think He doesn't care about us. If your parents didn't pay attention to you when were a child, you may have learned to expect rejection from those who are important to you. If you've ever lived with a spouse or a roommate who seldom spoke to you, you may have learned to expect silence from others. You might think that if the people you cared about had nothing to say to you, why on earth would the Creator of the universe be interested in speaking to you?

God isn't like your grouchy spouse, your silent roommate, or your stoic parent who never had much to say. He isn't hiding from you because He hates you. It isn't true that He has favorites, or that He doesn't want to spend time with you. He wants to connect with you every day. If there is anything preventing you from knowing God more intimately, it is on your side of the relationship, not His.

How do we learn to meet with God? Let's take a lesson from someone who walked with Him daily:

> *By an act of faith, Enoch skipped death completely. "They looked all over and couldn't find him because God had taken him." We know on the basis of reliable testimony that before he was taken "he pleased God." It's impossible to please God apart from faith. And why? Because anyone who wants to approach God must believe both that he exists and that he cares enough to respond to those who seek him.*
> HEB. 11:5-6 MSG

To get your parents attention you may have had to do your chores or clean your room. Others may have expected you to do favors for them. People usually require us to jump through hoops in order to earn their favor. But that isn't true of God. Enoch's walk with God was simply a matter of *faith*. If you want to be intimately involved in God's plans and want to know Him as a friend, the first step is to *believe* that He exists and that He cares enough to speak to you. For many of us, that means changing the way in which we think of Him.

The thing that prevented me from meeting with and hearing from God for the first 38 years of my life was unbelief and skepticism. I chose not to believe He existed, that He cared about me, or that I could know Him. That was a choice I made. But the moment I made a different choice—the choice to believe that He existed, that I could know Him, and that He could be heard—His voice was as easy to hear as that of anyone else. My choice to *believe* is what allowed me to draw near to Him.

We must choose to believe He wants to speak with us. While it would be ideal to know with absolute certainty that what we're seeing, feeling, or hearing is from God, the kingdom doesn't work that way. Everything we do that pertains to God is done by faith. We walk by faith in and through all of our experiences with Him. Faith is trusting that we're hearing His voice. Not knowing for *sure* that it's Him, but *trusting* that it's Him, in spite of any uncertainty we might have. "Faith" can be a nebulous term. You might wonder what this *faith* is that's required to walk with God. There are a couple of other words I use to describe faith. One word I use interchangeably with faith is *confidence*.

When we worry that God doesn't care about us, we're making a choice to entertain these thoughts, rather than entertaining other thoughts. If we want to communicate with God, we need to change our patterns of thinking—this is the true meaning of repentance. Rather than believing that He doesn't care or isn't going to speak to us, we need to change our mind and choose to believe that He does care and will speak to us. We need to become *confident* that His promise to speak to us is true. Faith is believing that we will receive what we've asked for.

The other word I sometimes use interchangeably for faith is *expectation*. If we want to connect with God, we must expect that He is going to speak to us. It is not presumptuous for us to expect this. He's already promised that He will. When we come to Him with the expectation of hearing His voice, we're simply choosing to believe that He will do what He promised. When we *expect* to hear God speak we'll recognize what He is saying with greater accuracy and we'll be less prone to doubt what He says.

One important factor that affects how well we hear God's voice is our desire. That is to say, the degree to which we want to be instructed by Him. The degree to which we sincerely want to hear His voice creates the terrain in our soul that receives communication from Him. The receptivity of our soul to His revelation is determined by how much we want to hear and follow what He tells us. This principle was explained by Jesus when the disciples asked why He spoke in parables. He said that He spoke in parables so that He might reveal the truth to those who had ears to hear it and at the same time conceal it from those who did not have ears to hear:

> "To you it has been given to know the mysteries of the kingdom of God, but to the rest it is given in parables, that 'Seeing they may not see, And hearing they may not understand.'"
> LK. 8:10

53

God desires to reveal the mysteries of the kingdom, but only to those who *desire* to receive them willingly and act upon what they receive. To those who have no desire to receive the things of the kingdom or act upon them, the truth is revealed, but it's revealed in a way that does not bear fruit. As Jesus said in the parable of the different types of soil, a person with this type of heart is like the hard ground, where the seed, after it is sown, is picked up by the birds of the air and carried away. God sows the seed upon all types of soil; He speaks to every type of heart. But hard ground cannot receive the seed. In the same way, a heart that is reluctant to hear the truth from God and act upon it cannot receive revelation and what is received doesn't bear fruit.

Jesus described a different type of soil which allowed the seed to germinate, but shortly afterward, weeds grew and crowded out the seed and it could not produce a harvest. He explained that the weeds were the cares of the world. They're the things that become distractions which divert our attention away from the revelation we receive from God. It's not even that these distractions are necessarily evil. Some of them are good things. But they're things we've placed out of priority. They are the people, events, hobbies, and concerns that we give our attention to, which divert our attention away from the things He shows us. If we don't give proper attention to the revelation He gives us and put it to use, it cannot bear fruit.

If for example, you have a series of dreams from God where you're praying for sick people in hospitals and nursing homes, it could be that God is calling you to go out into your community and pray for the sick. But if you allow your time to be used in other ways, such as hosting neighborhood meetings and coaching little league baseball, these things can become the weeds that choke out the seed, which prevents revelation from bearing fruit.

Jesus said in the parable of the talents, to those who make good use of what they've been given, they will be given more. But to those who have little, if they do not make good use of it, what little they have will be taken from them. The key to receiving more revelation from God is to make use of what He has given you. One reason why some people seem to receive so little revelation from God is that they've done nothing with what they've received.

For several years I hosted an open forum on a social network where people could receive prophetic words from God. There were a few people who came to receive a new prophetic word every day. I wonder at the wisdom of this approach to receiving revelation, which is common in Charismatic and Pentecostal circles. We seem to be fascinated with the idea of receiving revelation from God, but many times we do nothing with what we've received. We aren't supposed to receive revelation just to have more information. Revelation from God is like a seed. Its purpose is to bear fruit. And everything that is revealed to us from God is something we become responsible for. I've found that when God gives me several dreams about a particular subject, if I don't act upon them, I tend to receive little or no revelation on those subjects in the future. But when I receive dreams on a subject and act upon them, I usually receive more dreams on that subject and when I act upon *those* dreams, I receive even more.

When God first began giving me dreams about praying for people to be healed, I acted upon them. Even though I prayed for several hundred people and no one was healed, I continued having dreams about healing. I tried my best to be obedient to what He wanted me to do. It was a bit frustrating at the time to keep praying for the sick and not seeing results, but God kept giving me dreams where the ones I prayed with were being healed. I felt that if I just kept at it, one day someone would be healed. As I persisted, I began seeing people healed and eventually, I saw most of the people I prayed with healed. As I've continued praying for healing, the revelation has continued and it's become broader in scope. While most of the dreams I had years ago were about physical healing, most of the dreams I have today are about healing emotional trauma and mental illness. Living by faith isn't always easy. Sometimes it's rather difficult, especially when it seems as if our efforts are not bearing fruit. But the more we do what God asks us to do, the more we will see fruit produced, and the more fruit we see, the more confident we'll become that we are truly hearing His voice.

Persistence

In Luke chapter 11 we find an important lesson taught by Jesus. After teaching His disciples how to pray, He taught them how to persist until they received what they asked for. I have many friends who hear God extremely well. Although they hear Him in very different ways, they all share one thing in common: Every one of them has remarkable persistence. Their determination and persistence is the thing that sets them apart from everyone else. They are leaders because they're successful and a large part of their success comes from their persistence. If you want to have the same kind of success they have you must develop the same kind of persistence they have.

In the society in which we live, we've grown accustomed to having what we want immediately. When I first set my mind to seeing visions, the changes in my spiritual vision came very slowly. And I'll admit, it was very frustrating. I sat in my ambulance with my eyes closed, hour after hour, day after day. I could have given up in frustration, but I wanted to see visions badly enough that quitting wasn't an option. Over the course of weeks and months, my ability to see visions gradually improved and today I see visions with ease.

I'd love to be able to guarantee that you'll have dramatic results in a few days or even in a few weeks. Unfortunately, for some people, it might take longer than a few weeks before they notice a significant change in their ability to discern God's voice or see visions. For some of us, the change will be instantaneous, but for others the process will be much longer. The recalibration of our spiritual senses might take a little longer than we'd like. I can't promise you a definite time period in which you'll notice changes, but I can assure you that if you're willing to stick with a regular routine of getting alone in a quiet place and being intentional about hearing God speak, you'll notice that He is speaking, however faintly His voice might seem.

Exercise

Set aside between 15 and 30 minutes for this exercise. Find a place that is free from noise and distractions and allows a comfortable way for you to sit or lie down. Have something ready to write with so that you can record the impressions you receive from God. Get comfortable and fix your mind on God. Expect that He is going to communicate something to you. If there are questions you'd like to ask, you might ask them to Him. After asking a question, wait for an answer which could come as an image in your mind, a thought impression, a sudden emotion, or some other change you sense that was not present before you asked the question. Make a mental note of any impressions you receive and ask follow up questions if you'd like. Write down the impressions you receive to make a permanent record of them. Writing down the revelation you receive serves a couple of purposes:

If you go through a time when it seems as if God isn't speaking very clearly, you can look back at what He told you in these exercises and see that He is really speaking to you.

Some of what you receive in these exercises will provide insights into His future plans for you. If you write them down it can serve as a kind of road map for your future. When the things that you wrote down come to pass, you can look back at how He showed you them in advance and it'll demonstrate His faithfulness to do what He said He would.

--- **Notes** ---

Notes

CHAPTER SEVEN

God's Not so Audible Voice

THERE ARE MANY PEOPLE WHO have heard God's voice very clearly. Some so clearly they've described it as sounding like an audible voice. If you've never heard God speak in such a voice, you might feel as if you've never actually heard Him speak at all. Don't worry. It's likely you have heard Him speak, but not in the way you expected. When we use the word *audible*, we're referring to a sound that is made which can be heard by anyone with normal hearing. If I were to strike a gong in the middle of a crowded auditorium, it's likely that everyone present would hear the audible sound made by the gong. An audible sound is not selective for certain people. Anyone who is present can hear a sound that is audible. When God speaks to someone in a way that is unusually loud, they may *perceive* the message to be one that was spoken in an audible voice. But unless others who are nearby are also able to hear the same voice and the same message, the voice was not an audible one, but something else.

When I speak to my wife, the sound she hears is the result of different forms of energy being transmitted through physical structures of the human body. In order for me to speak in a voice that can be heard (which is the definition of an audible voice) my lungs must exhale air through a set of vocal cords that stretch and contract to form sound waves, which are shaped by my mouth. The sound waves travel through the air and are picked up by her ear drum. The structures in her ear transmit the sound waves and change them into an electrical signal which is carried to her brain through the auditory nerve. Her brain processes the signal and converts it into the audible voice of her husband.

God is a Spirit. Spirit beings do not have physical structures like ear drums and vocal cords. His voice is not a wave of sound that comes from His lungs. It does not travel through our ear drum to our auditory nerve and then to our brain. Even though it may *seem* to some as if they're hearing an audible voice like any other human voice, spirits do not have the physical structures of communication required to create audible speech. Spiritual communication uses a completely different set of senses. It is done primarily through the transmission of thought impressions (and impressions via other spiritual senses) directly from spirit to spirit. These impressions bypass the physical structures of the human body.

When God speaks to the person sitting next to you in a restaurant, you can't hear what He is saying, but they can. This is because spirits have the ability to direct their messages to specific targets, while concealing them from those who are nearby. If spirit beings communicated in ways that relied on the structures of the physical body, everyone nearby would hear them speaking just as clearly as the one they were speaking to. They also have the ability to manifest their appearance to only certain individuals, while remaining invisible to others.

God speaks to us through spiritual language because it is the only way in which spirits are able to communicate. Spiritual communication is easy for our spirits to sense, but it is impossible for our physical bodies to sense. Because there are two different types of communication we must sense and interpret, God gave us a third component with the ability to receive both forms of communication. This third part of our being, the soul, is the bridge that ties the spiritual and the physical together.

God gave us a soul for many purposes. It is commonly believed to be the seat of the mind, the will, and the emotions. It is also the part of our being where input from the physical and spiritual worlds are received and interpreted. The soul is able to process all the input from the various physical senses of sight, hearing, touch, taste, and smell, as well as the entire range of human emotions. And in the same way that it processes these senses from the physical body, it is able to receive and interpret these same senses from the spiritual body. God, angels, and demons can all be sensed through a set of spiritual senses nearly identical to the ones the physical body has. For those who have difficulty recognizing spiritual beings and the things they communicate, the problem is that their soul has not been conditioned to recognize this kind of communication. The exercises provided at the end of the chapters are intended to train the soul to become more sensitive to spiritual communication.

It's common when we first recognize that God is speaking to us to sense Him as a voice of gentle correction. He speaks to our conscience to help us develop patterns of thinking and acting that are in accordance with His character. As children, the development of godly character is a primary focus, but as we grow more mature, there are other things we need to learn. It is God's desire for us to understand and manifest our true identity.

The world tends to shape us into its own mold through interactions that we have with friends, parents, and teachers. The world has an identity it would like us to conform to, but God has a very different one that He has created for us. The identity He has prepared for us is sometimes in direct opposition to the one the world wants us to accept. One of the most important parts of our spiritual growth is rejecting a wrong identity the world may have given us, and receiving the one God has given us.

The world may tell you that you're a failure, but God will tell you that in time, you'll be a success. The world may tell you that you have no creative talent, but God will show you the specific talents He has placed inside you. The world may tell you that no one cares about you. The Spirit of God will tell you that heaven rejoices at even your most feeble accomplishment. The world may tell you that you are not lovable. God will tell you that He has always loved you from the very beginning and He will never stop loving you. The world may tell you that you are acceptable only as long as your behavior is acceptable. God wants you to know that no amount of mistakes or failures can ever diminish the acceptance He has for you. The world may tell you that you are on your own. God will tell you that He has hundreds of angels waiting to assist you in your divinely ordained destiny. God reveals these things to us in a variety of ways. Some of it may be revealed through prophetic words from others. Some will be revealed through dreams or visions. But much of it will be revealed through the personal conversations you have with Him.

CHAPTER EIGHT

Is It God or Is It Me?

ONE CONCERN YOU MIGHT HAVE about hearing God's voice is whether something you heard originated in your own mind or the mind of God. For some, there is too much uncertainty over knowing the origin of an idea that they prefer not to attempt to discern what God might be saying, for fear of being wrong. Determining the origin of revelation may seem like a daunting task, but there are a few simple steps we can take that will help us verify the source of any revelation.

A few of the ways in which God speaks to us are visions, dreams, aromas, emotions, skin sensations, and thought impressions that carry messages to our mind. (In the next section we'll look at these modes of communication separately.) It's common for us to attribute these things to an over-active imagination. But here's the thing I've noticed about God's messages that helps me distinguish them from the workings of my own mind:

The believer has two spirits living inside them—their own spirit and the Spirit of God. These two spirits are the sources of two different kinds of thought or streams of revelation. Before we can know which thoughts are God's we must first know which belong to us. One problem many of us have is that we do not know our own thoughts the way we should. When we know ourselves well and understand clearly the ways in which our mind works, we can view our own thoughts like an objective observer. The better we know our own thoughts, the easier it is to discern the thoughts that are not ours, but God's, or those of a demon. The first step in learning to distinguish our thoughts from God's is becoming more aware of the nature of our own thought life.

In the more than half a century I've walked the earth I've come to know myself pretty well. I've learned to recognize the ways in which my own mind thinks. If someone copied and pasted one of my articles into an e-mail and sent it to me I would recognize it as mine. If someone hung one of my paintings on the wall of a restaurant, I would recognize the artist as myself. I recognize my own thoughts and the visual material of my own mind when I see them. And when I hear a thought that is unfamiliar to my way of thinking, I also recognize it as being "not from me." When I see a visual image that is foreign to my own creativity I recognize it as being "not mine."

While the thoughts of mortals are different, they are more or less of equal quality. The thoughts of God however, are infinitely higher and distinctly different from our own. God's thoughts are so much more sublime than my thoughts. They are full of love, life, wisdom, compassion, and mercy. Although I would like to think that my thoughts are like this, if I am honest with myself, I must admit that God's thoughts carry a certain quality that my thoughts do not have. If we're going to discern God's thoughts from ours we must learn to be honest with ourselves about our thoughts. Otherwise we deceive ourselves and we can't hope to distinguish God's thoughts from our own.

We know that every good and perfect thing comes down from the Father of Lights (Jas. 1:17). Everything that is good in the world has its origin in God. I would like to think that the good thoughts I have originated in my own mind. But when I have a thought that is full of love or compassion or mercy—even though the thought *seems* to have sprung forth from within my own mind, I must conclude that it could not have come from me. I know its source must be the mind of God—for that is the origin of everything that is good and perfect.

We must remember that although God's voice is external to us, His Spirit resides in us. Because of this, when He speaks, we perceive His *external* voice to be an *internal* experience. We perceive His thoughts as our own thoughts. The way in which His thoughts come to us is so subtle it's often hard to recognize that they had their origin outside of us. But these brilliant, loving, compassionate thoughts are the thoughts of God being spoken by the Holy Spirit. The same is true for visual images that we receive from Him. Many times we think an image came from our imagination, when it actually came from God. Half the battle of knowing that what you're seeing, feeling, or hearing is from God is simply a matter of knowing that it isn't from you.

Confirmation of the things we believe we've heard from God is important. But how do we begin to know if something is from God or from another source?

Our soul creates its own messages, including thoughts, impressions, emotions, and visual images. One difference between the ones that come from an external source and ones that come from our soul is that those which come from an external source are difficult or impossible to manipulate or change willfully. A message that is external to us cannot be changed by us. Whereas a message that originates in our soul can be changed by exerting our will over it.

There is another way in which we can distinguish the origin of revelation, but it is different (and contrary) to the way that is taught by many church leaders. Many people teach that anything we believe we've heard from God must line up with scripture in order for us to know with certainty that it's from God. If it does not line up with scripture, they say, we must toss it out. There's nothing wrong with searching the scriptures to see if something has a biblical basis, but many of the things God will reveal to us cannot be verified by the scriptures. I've had God speak to me about accepting a new job, turning down opportunities to speak at various churches, and many other personal issues, none of which could be conclusively verified by scripture alone.

A wise person takes their decisions before God and asks for His input. But whether something came from the heart of God or some other place is not determined by its inclusion in the Bible. The origin of wisdom and the source of any revelation can best be determined by evaluating the fruit it produces. Jesus taught that a polluted stream does not give pure water and that you do not gather grapes from thorn bushes or figs from thistles. The source of anything is always best determined by examining the fruit that it bears. False teachers and evil spirits can quote the scriptures, but the fruit that a thing produces will always reveal its source.

The Holy Spirit is called the Comforter, the Spirit of Grace, the Spirit of Peace, the Spirit of Wisdom, and the Spirit of Truth, because these are the things that His words produce. If anyone hears the words of the Spirit and acts on them, the same fruit will be produced in their life. The voice of the Spirit produces the fruit of the Spirit, which is love, joy, peace, longsuffering, kindness, goodness, faithfulness, gentleness, and self-control (Gal. 5:22). So if a person says they are hearing from God, and they act upon what they have heard, but the fruit produced is condemnation, fear, discord or any other negative quality, we can tell that this person was not hearing from God. I transport mentally ill patients frequently who hear voices that speak condemning and cruel words to them. These people often think they are hearing God's voice. I know that in most cases they are not hearing from God, because the fruit that comes from what they hear is not the fruit of the Spirit. These people tend to be filled with self-hatred, fear, anxiety, envy, and other attitudes that are inconsistent with the fruit of the Spirit.

You might receive an impression from God that you should speak to a neighbor about their marital problems. If you speak to them and learn that their marriage is in trouble and God gives you counsel that you share with them which saves their marriage—the revelation you received is confirmed. You were hearing from God. If on the other hand, you find that your neighbors are not having marriage problems, you may have not been hearing from God. The fruit of any revelation testifies of its source.

My friend Shae Bynes once organized a retreat for entrepreneurs. She asked God what the theme for the retreat would be and she received no answer. She received many prompts from Him about logistics, but she registered attendees without telling them what they would be learning. As the time for the retreat drew near, she became concerned as she still didn't know what the retreat would be about. She recalled the day that God finally told her what the agenda would be:

> "I went to the hair salon to get my hair done and after my appointment my husband asked me to meet him at Office Max. I drove over to Office Max, turned the car off, and was just about to open the car door when I felt a heartache unlike I had ever felt before. I started to cry uncontrollably... I didn't even know why I was crying. My hair was looking fabulous and I was in a great mood just moments earlier. All I knew was at that moment my heart hurt... a lot."

Shae doesn't suffer from depression, yet she sobbed for what felt like no reason. She had never felt these kinds of emotions before. She contacted her business partner who suggested it might be a prophetic message about the subject of the retreat. During their chat, God revealed that the attendees would be delivered from bitterness and unforgiveness. At the retreat, she explained to the attendees that God wanted them to go through a process of forgiving people (former business associates as well as family members) for the pains they had caused them. The retreat turned into a mass exercise in deliverance and emotional healing.

Shae would never have known if the emotions she felt were really from God and if her interpretation of them was correct if she had not taken the risk of delivering a very unusual message to the group. The fact that the attendees responded to the message en masse, was the fruit that testified to the origin of the revelation. The kingdom of God is advanced when we take risks. Taking risks is one of the best ways we can learn to know if and how we are hearing from God. As we obey the revelation we receive and act upon it, producing fruit, we'll grow in confidence that we're hearing accurately from God.

PART TWO
How God Speaks

CHAPTER NINE

Spiritual Abilities versus Spiritual Gifts

IN THIS SECTION, PART TWO, we will explore the many ways in which God speaks to everyone, universally. All the ways of communication we'll cover in this section involve our innate spiritual *senses*—and not spiritual *gifts*. Our innate spiritual senses are ones we have which we can use independently. They do not require God's empowerment in order for them to function. There are some common misconceptions about how these senses function, so I'll illustrate the difference between innate spiritual abilities and spiritual gifts.

An ability is a skill or sense that can be used without special empowerment from God. An example is the ability to see. Except in cases of blindness, we are all born with the innate ability to see with our physical eyes. As a newborn, things that are near to us appear in focus, though a newborn has difficulty focusing on distant objects. We're not usually born with our abilities fully-developed. We must practice using them before they operate at their fullest potential. The same is true for the rest of our senses—both physical and spiritual—we're born with them intact, they must be developed, and their use is not dependent upon God.

By contrast, a gift speaks of something we *cannot* do ourselves. When God grants us the ability to do something we could not ordinarily do, it is considered to be a gift. An example is the gift of speaking in tongues. This gift is not an innate skill we are born with that can be developed. We refer to it as a "gift" because it cannot be done except by the power of God.

Before we discuss the details of how we develop our spiritual senses, we should discuss the reasons why they are important. If you're a Christian, the terms we're about to discuss will be familiar to you, but if you are not, please don't be offended or feel as if this discussion is not relevant to you. It is relevant. As you begin to recognize that God is speaking to you, eventually you're going to want to know what to do with what He tells you. Much of what we do with the revelation we receive pertains to the spiritual gifts we're going to study in the last section of this book, Part Three. At this point we should briefly touch on some of those spiritual gifts.

The gifts of the Holy Spirit are ways in which the Spirit of God operates through us in order to speak to or in some way interact with those around us. There are nine different gifts of the Holy Spirit mentioned in the Bible. Several of them involve hearing, seeing, or sensing revelation from God in some way. Some in the church have taught that the gifts of the Spirit will operate in us effectively before we've had time to develop our spiritual senses. But in fact the opposite is true. We must first develop our ability to hear, see, and sense what God is saying and then we can operate in the gifts of the Spirit. I aim to teach you first how to hone your spiritual senses. In Part Three we'll look at how those senses can be used through the gifts of the Spirit.

The spiritual gifts generally require us to develop our spiritual senses before they function effectively. The gift of discerning of spirits mentioned in 1 Cor. 12:10 is a good example. The discerning of spirits can be done in a number of ways. Some people smell the presence of spirits such as angels or demons, while others can see them. The revelation of the presence of such spirits is dependent on our spiritual senses, not our natural ones. If you're not sensing spiritual activity through one of your spiritual senses, it is probably because that sense is presently in an undeveloped state. Exercise is the best way to make the spiritual senses more sensitive. Some people know spirits are present because the Holy Spirit reveals them through thought impressions or visions. Some people "feel" or "sense" the presence of spirits. This is sometimes described as a sudden, overwhelming sense of fear or dread when an evil spirit draws near, or a sense of peace or joy when an angel is nearby.

If God intends for you to operate in the gift of discerning of spirits by seeing the spirits that are around you, it will require you to develop your ability to see in the spirit first. If He wants to reveal them through words that you hear as thoughts in your mind, you need to develop your ability to discern those thoughts. While the control of a spiritual gift is subject to the operation of the Holy Spirit, the development of an ability is under our control. Abilities are honed and perfected through practice and they lie undeveloped when we ignore them. If we never develop our ability to see in the spirit or hear God's voice, the operation of the gift of discerning of spirits can be hindered.

The writer of the book of Hebrews spoke about the need for them to grow in spiritual maturity:

> *"For though by this time you ought to be teachers, you need someone to teach you again the first principles of the oracles of God; and you have come to need milk and not solid food. For everyone who partakes only of milk is unskilled in the word of righteousness, for he is a babe. But solid food belongs to those who are of full age, that is, those who by reason of use have their senses exercised to discern both good and evil."*
> HEB. 5:12-24

The author pointed out that although these believers should have been teaching others by this time, they were still spiritually immature. He contrasted their immaturity with those who had grown into maturity, noting that maturity comes by exercising our senses. Anyone can develop spiritual maturity and their spiritual senses through exercise and practice.

I'd like to share a word of caution:

It's become popular to categorize people according to the most common way in which they receive revelation from God. Some people have taken on identifiers such as "feeler," "hearer," "seer," and other labels that describe the way in which they receive revelation from God. While it can be helpful to identify particular modes of receiving revelation, identifying ourselves by these terms may have unintended consequences. If for example, you accept the term "seer" as your identity, you may subconsciously block your ability to receive revelation through the other senses, believing they are not part of your identity and not one of the ways in which God speaks to you. Even if you do not block those impressions from God, you may not expect them. And when you do sense them you might attribute them to something other than God. Be aware of this tendency and don't limit your ability to hear from God by a label you've accepted.

CHAPTER TEN

Visions

JUST AS WITH ALL THE other ways in which God communicates with us, visions are accessible to everyone, even if we believe we have never seen one before. There are some who would suggest that visions are a gift that is given only to a few special individuals, but this idea is neither biblical, nor is it fully supported by the testimony of those who see visions.

Not every person is born with a healthy pair of physical eyes. Some are born without them due to birth defects. But every human spirit ever created has a pair of spiritual eyes. And in the same way that we need to exercise our physical eyes in order to develop better clarity of our natural vision, we must exercise our spiritual eyes in order to see things in the spiritual world. God is always speaking to His creation, and much of what He says is communicated through visual imagery. Since many of us have never seen a vision—or at least not one that we were aware of—it's common to think He is not speaking to us in this way. The problem is not that He isn't speaking. The problem is that He is a Spirit who speaks in a spiritual language that is received by our spirit, and many of us have not developed our ability to recognize the visual spiritual language He uses. We've had our spiritual senses dulled by sensory input from the physical world, which makes it difficult to recognize input from the spiritual one. The key to perceiving and understanding spiritual communication is to have our spiritual senses trained and refocused.

Anyone can see visions from God, and in fact, we receive revelation from Him in the form of visions every day. But many times we attribute the images our mind receives to our imagination, or we fail to perceive them at all. Most of us need to have our spiritual senses trained and our soul conditioned to recognize visual images. A few people are born with a very sharp ability to recognize things they see in the spiritual world. It's my belief that some are born this way so that they might help others who need to have their spiritual senses trained.

In August of 2008, God appeared to me in a dream and said He was going to show me what was wrong with my patients, and that if I prayed for them, He would heal them. Prior to that night, I had never seen a vision, or at least not one I was aware of. I wasn't born with a fully-developed ability to see visions, and I didn't know how God was going to show me what was wrong with my patients. But I wanted to see the things He wanted to show me. I needed to take a little initiative and allow my spiritual senses to be trained.

God is a relational being. It's impossible to have a meaningful relationship with Him if you won't devote the time needed to develop the relationship. I've noticed that when I desire to spend more time with Him, He always finds a way to free up time in my schedule. God gave me some free time at work so that I might use it to get to know Him better, and in the process develop my ability to see visions. If you want to develop this ability and grow closer to God, you'll need to find some time in which to do it. Some people have large blocks of time every day or several times a week to spend with God, but not everyone does. It isn't necessary to devote an hour or two every day to be alone with God. If you can only spend 15 minutes a day focusing on Jesus and what He wants to reveal to you—it can make a huge difference.

I spent my time in the ambulance between calls with my eyes closed. During these times I quieted my soul and did my best to block out distractions from the world around me. (Although it's possible to see visions with your eyes open, I found it easier to block out distracting background images by keeping my eyes closed.) I focused my heart on God and gave Him all of my attention. For the first few days that I did this, I saw very little in the way of visions, but as time went on, I gradually began seeing faintly detectable images appear in my mind's eye. There was nothing dramatic about the process. Everything happened very gradually.

One of the most common misunderstandings about visions is the idea that they appear to be external to us. Sometimes a vision may appear to be an external reality, but most times it will appear in the same way any other visual image appears in our mind—through our imagination. God uses the same apparatus to show us a vision that we use to imagine in our mind what our husband or wife may be doing at work. This is the reason many people write off revelation from God as being "just their imagination."

At first, the images I saw in my mind were blurry and two-dimensional in appearance. They were mostly images of famous people that I recognized. I was excited to finally be seeing visions, but soon my excitement turned to frustration, because I didn't understand what any of the images meant. God doesn't give us visions for our entertainment. They're usually an invitation to a discussion. Revelation is a two-way street. We need to respond to what He reveals to us so a dialogue can take place. When you see an image in your mind or when a thought impression arises out of nowhere and you think it might be from Him, you might begin a discussion by asking Him what it means.

I began a discussion (in my mind) with God about the images He showed me. The dialogue consisted of me thinking thoughts in my mind in response to the images I saw. This might seem a little strange if you're not acquainted with speaking to God through thoughts, but this is the most common way in which people have conversations with Him. He seldom speaks to us in a loud, booming voice. It's normally done through barely perceptible thought impressions. And since that's how He speaks to us, we can speak to Him in the same way. It might seem silly at first, but with practice, you'll quickly become more comfortable with this process.

As I closed my eyes, I would see an image appear. At first, the images were slow to take shape in my mind, but the more I did these exercises, the faster they appeared. I would silently tell God (in my mind) what I thought an image represented. If I guessed correctly about the meaning, the image would disappear and another one would take its place. If I guessed incorrectly, the image would remain there and I would take another guess at its meaning. Some images required many guesses before I was able to correctly identify what they meant. Some were easy to guess on the first try. Through this process of guessing what each image meant, God was training my spiritual eyes to receive revelation, He was training my mind to display the images accurately, and He was training my spirit to understand the visual language He wanted me to learn.

As time went on, the images I saw became more sharply focused, and the intensity of the colors was more vivid than what I was able to see even with my physical eyes. The colors of the spiritual realm are nearly infinite. The more you develop your ability to see in the spirit, the more you'll notice increasing intensity and variety of color. Some of the images I saw were translucent in appearance. In the spiritual world, many things—heavenly ones in particular—radiate a kind of light that is not present in the physical world. As I practiced seeing in the spirit, some of the images I saw became three-dimensional and I saw multiple scenes that overlapped and eventually the images began to move. Some of the scenes I saw were animated cartoons. These visions are something like watching a video in your mind. Moving images and scenes that appear as videos are able to convey a greater depth of meaning than a single image.

The best way to develop your spiritual vision is practice. You may notice improvement immediately, but not everyone does. Be patient with the process. It may take months or even years in some cases. What you should notice is that as you continue to exercise your spiritual eyes, there will be subtle improvements each time. If you persist, before long, you'll have spiritual eyes that can see better than your physical ones. The key to seeing with greater accuracy is practice.

Exercise

Sit or lie down in a comfortable position. Close your eyes and fix your attention on God. As you do this, try to detect any images, however faint they are, that appear in your mind and make note of them. Look to see if the images move or change shape and make note of what they do. Ask God questions about what you see. (You can do this aloud or by thinking the questions in your mind.) Ask Him to interpret or explain the images you see and journal whatever you hear Him say. This exercise can be repeated daily.

Notes

Dreams

FOR THOUSANDS OF YEARS, MEN and women have understood how God uses dreams to speak to us. In some Arab cultures, the villagers gather together each morning to discuss their dreams. A key part of the community's planning is done in accordance with the dreams people have had.

Members of the Islamic faith, for example, don't expect their distant God to speak back to them personally. But they do ask for guidance through their dreams. It has been well-documented in recent years that thousands of Muslims have been visited by Jesus in dreams and visions where He told them He was the truth they had been seeking. Thousands of converts to Christianity have come because God is speaking to people through dreams in places where possessing a Bible is illegal. Through dreams, even militant Muslims have been inspired to believe in Jesus as more than just a prophet, as He is acknowledged in Islam.

In the book of Job, Elihu reminded Job that because we often fail to perceive God's voice while we're awake, He reveals secrets in our sleep:

> *"For God may speak in one way, or in another, yet man does not perceive it. In a dream, in a vision of the night, when deep sleep falls upon men, while slumbering on their beds, then He opens the ears of men, and seals their instruction. In order to turn man from his deed, and conceal pride from man, He keeps back his soul from the pit, and his life from perishing by the sword."*
> JOB 33:14-18

The Bible says:

> *"It's the glory of God to conceal a matter, and the glory of kings to search a matter out."*
> PROV. 25:2

Many people take what they perceive to be God's silence as His indifference toward us. But God is not indifferent toward us. If He wanted, He could manifest His voice so clearly that everyone would hear Him perfectly. But a God who is so clearly evident is one who would remove much of our freedom, including the freedom to ignore Him if we wish. God is not so intrusive as to barge into the life of someone who would rather not be troubled by Him. He is a gentleman and He does not intrude where He is not wanted. In order that He might allow us the liberty to ignore Him, He has chosen to conceal Himself to a large degree. It is the glory of God to conceal His affairs—not so that He cannot be found, but so that those who earnestly desire to know Him will seek and find Him.

Part of the hidden nature of God is that He speaks veiled mysteries to us through dreams. What kind of mysteries does He reveal? I have a dream journal I've been keeping for the last eight years. In it are more than 300 dreams on the subject of healing alone. Some of the dreams revealed things about healing that are not clearly explained in the Bible. I believe the Bible is a great place to learn the basics and from which to build foundational principles, but many of the details of subjects like healing and deliverance are discovered as we operate in them and as God gives us keys to greater effectiveness through dreams.

Daniel and Joseph were both skilled in dream interpretation and because of it, were promoted to positions of power under the rulers of their respective lands. Both men said that dreams and their interpretations came from God (see Gen. 40:8 and Dan. 2:28). The Bible is full of accounts where God spoke through dreams. Here are a few examples:

In Genesis 28, Jacob fell asleep by a river. God came to him in a dream and gave him several covenant promises: to bless him all of his days, to make a great family for him, to give him the land promised to Isaac and Abraham, and that all the nations of the world would be blessed through him.

Joseph's cell-mates had divine dreams; one of them was promised freedom; the other was warned of his impending death (see Gen. 40:5).

Pharaoh was warned in a dream about a coming famine that would last seven years (see Gen. 41).

God appeared to Solomon in a dream while he slept, and told him to ask for anything he wanted. In the conversation, Solomon asked for wisdom to rule over God's people. God gave him wisdom greater than anyone who ever lived. He also received great honor, riches, and a promise of long life if he would be obedient. When Solomon woke up he realized all these things happened while he was sleeping (see 1 Kgs. 3:5-15).

King Nebuchadnezzar was given a dream concerning his own kingdom and all the kingdoms to follow. It was revealed that his kingdom was the greatest of the kingdoms of man. He was greatly encouraged by this dream (see Dan. 2:36-45).

When Joseph learned that his wife Mary was pregnant, he considered leaving her, but an angel came to him in a dream and revealed that her pregnancy was a divine miracle and that he was to fulfill his marriage commitment. He was also warned in a dream of Herod's plan to kill Jesus and he was told to flee to Egypt. The accounts are recorded in Matthew chapters 1 & 2.

If you're not having dreams right now, there are a couple of things you can do that might help you receive them. Many Arabs have dreams from

God and in some cases, appearances from Jesus, because they highly value their dreams. God tends to speak to us through the things we *value* most. One key to receiving revelation is having a healthy desire for the things of God. By "healthy desire" I mean that it is primarily motivated by a strong longing to know Him better. Our motives are extremely important. If we want to have dreams just so that we can impress our friends with them, we're seeking them for the wrong reason. If we desire to see angels because we feel like it will make us more important in the eyes of our friends or family, we are again asking from a wrong motive.

The issue that lies beneath wrong motives is usually a wounded soul that feels inferior, unacceptable, or unloved. The solution is to have the wounds in your soul healed and to develop a better understanding of how much God values you. When you truly understand how much He loves you and what your real identity is in Him, those self-serving motives will be a thing of the past.

To receive dreams from God, ask Him for dreams every night. It also helps to keep some kind of record of the dreams you have. Your dream journal can be a notebook with blank pages, a pile of blank note cards, a digital voice recorder, or whatever works for you. I keep a couple of pens, a small flashlight, and a few 3 x 5 index cards on my nightstand. I record my dreams on the cards, then every few months, I transfer them to a word processing document on my computer. I take my dreams very seriously. Part of growing in spiritual maturity is learning to be a good steward of the revelation you receive.

Dreams can come from three different sources. Some dreams come from God, some originate in our soul, and some come from the enemy. Dreams from God can be received directly from the Holy Spirit, Jesus, or from angels. Dreams from the enemy are usually sent by evil spirits of various kinds. Dreams that originate in our soul tend to be a way in which our mind processes our activities and thoughts of that day.

I'm reluctant to give rules for discerning the origin of a dream. Applying rules too rigidly can lead you to dismiss a dream from God as one that was from the enemy. But it can be helpful to keep a couple of things in mind when analyzing a dream:

Dreams from our soul often have a disjointed feeling to them and the scenes seem to have a random quality with very little continuity.

Dreams from the enemy often have dark colors in them that are prominent. They tend to cause us to feel fear, shame, condemnation, lust, inadequacy, and other negative emotions that are not consistent with the nature of God.

Dreams from God tend to speak to us about familiar situations. They're usually instructive or encouraging, though they can contain warnings, correction, direction in a career, information about personal finances, information about spiritual gifting, information about relationships, and just about any other part of life.

Most people tend to have dreams that are highly symbolic. For this reason, it's good to become familiar with the symbolic imagery of dreams. The best source to help decode the images you find in dreams is the Bible. When you have a dream, write it down in as much detail as you can. Most dreams—even ones that seem terribly complex—can be summarized in a few sentences. Sometimes it isn't possible to write every detail. Don't worry if you miss some of the minor details. I've had many lengthy dreams with details too numerous to write down in the middle of the night. In those cases, I generally try to capture the main elements of the dream.

The setting of a dream and places that are mentioned can be very important. I once had a dream where I registered for a conference in Corpus Christi, Texas. After looking for conferences in Corpus Christi for several weeks, one day it dawned on me that *Corpus Christi* is Latin for the *body of Christ*. It was then that I realized the dream was speaking of my ministry to the followers of Christ, and not about attending a literal conference.

Make note of any numbers that appear in a dream, any colors that are prominent, spoken messages that seem significant, and the names of people. Sometimes the main message of a dream can be determined by looking up the meaning of the name of the main person who appears in the dream. Sometimes the meaning of their first name is the main message God is trying to get across. You might have a recurring dream where a friend named Abigail appears. How comforting would it be if you were to look up the meaning of her Hebrew name and find that it means "the Father's joy?"

If the person who appears or is mentioned in a dream is known to you for a specific gift or talent, or is an expert in a certain field, the message may indicate that you have a similar calling as them. During the months I spent writing this book there was a period of several weeks where all of my dreams involved C. S. Lewis. In these dreams, God was encouraging me to keep my focus on writing. I've had dreams where other well-known people were featured prominently or gave me messages. In those dreams, God illustrated that I have similar *calling* or assignment to theirs.

The emotions we feel in a dream are a good indicator of the source of the dream and its interpretation. Many people have dreams where they're attending the funeral of a friend or relative. Often, they have a great sense of peace in the dream, which they would not have if they were actually attending the funeral. When we have a strong sense of peace in a dream, it's an indicator of a couple of things: First, it strongly suggests that the dream is from God and not the enemy or our soul. Peace is a fruit of the Spirit of God (see Gal 5:22). It's one way by which we can know that revelation had its origin in God. Second, a sense of peace suggests that the dream is symbolic and not literal. If the dream portrayed a literal death, we would not expect peace to be the dominant emotion. Death can speak of many other things; often it's used symbolically to portray spiritual transformation. If the person whose funeral you're attending is about to go through a process of spiritual growth, it may be portrayed to you as you attending their funeral. Symbolically, you're witnessing the death of their old life and the beginning of their new one.

Look up the biblical significance of any numbers that appear in a dream. They usually hold clues to help you decode the message. Many times the numbers you see in a dream will point you to a Bible verse that God wants to speak to you through.

Unfortunately, there isn't space in this book to give a comprehensive treatment of dreams and their interpretation. I would, however, like to encourage you to ask God to speak to you through dreams and when you receive them, know that they are love letters from your heavenly Father.

Exercise

If you're not having dreams from God, it may help to develop a bedtime practice of asking Him for dreams, expecting to receive them, and then journaling the ones you receive. I have many friends who have found that as they take their dream life more seriously, they tend to have more dreams and more important ones. As you're getting ready to sleep, ask God for a dream that reveals something He wants you to know. When you have a dream, as soon as you wake up, write down as much of it as you can recall. Don't wait—because the dream may be easily forgotten. Each night, ask for a dream from God and write down every dream you have. During the daytime hours, think about the dreams you've had and ask God to help you interpret them. I've found many times, as my wife and I discuss a particular dream, He'll give one of us the interpretation.

Notes

CHAPTER TWELVE

Nature

IT'S OFTEN BEEN SAID THAT God speaks to us powerfully, yet gently through nature. Even some agnostics will admit that they feel most at peace and perhaps even sense the presence of God when hiking alone in the wilderness. Most of the time, when people say God speaks to them through nature, they're describing the fact that they've felt unusually inspired by a sunset or noticed a prophetic symbol in the clouds. I've had these experiences myself.

One morning right around daybreak, as I drove to work, I noticed the unmistakable figure of a lion in the clouds. He had a regal and majestic appearance and seeing him in the clouds calmed my nerves, which had been frazzled by things that were going on at work. That morning I had a great sense of peace and comfort come over me as I focused my thoughts on the lion of the tribe of Judah who seemed to be dutifully watching over my affairs.

A friend of mine shared a story about the time she was led to send me a gift of money, which was confirmed to her in an unusual way. Here is her explanation of how God spoke to her:

> I was having a chat with the Lord on my daily walk around the lake. We were chatting about giving and tithing. I had some money put aside to give earlier in the month. I said to the Lord, "Do you want me to give this money to the church or do you want me to give it to someone else?"
>
> He said, "Put your money at the feet of the apostles."
>
> Immediately your name popped into my head. I said to the Lord, "Okay that is different than what I was expecting, so I would like you to give me confirmation." So an idea popped into my head and I thought: if I see a deer walking across my path today I know it is you, Lord.
>
> I kept walking and when I turned the corner, there in front of me was a small muntjac deer. He stood in the middle of the path and looked at me and then trotted away. Now, you might not think that is an unusual thing in your part of the world, but I have lived here for 14 years and have been at that lake thousands of times and I have never seen a deer there—ever! I'm not sure why the deer request popped into my head, but the Lord obviously wanted you to have the money. So be very blessed today.

I'd like to illustrate how God speaks specific revelation to us through nature by sharing an unusual experience I had several years ago. My friend who is the editor of the website *Northwest Prophetic* had been receiving a lot of prophetic words about changes God had planned for the Church that was represented in dreams and visions people were having where they saw a tsunami. He asked me to inquire of God and ask if He would give me the revelation I would need to write a prophetic word on that subject. At first, the idea seemed a bit odd. I'd never considered asking God for specific revelation that could be used to write a prophetic word to the church. But I asked God if He had anything to share on the subject and a short time later my request was granted in an unusual way.

My kids and I spent a lot of time in Long Beach, Washington when they were young. One day we spent a day at the beach when the moon was full and the forecast was for higher than normal surf. We took our wet suits and boards expecting to have a blast in the big waves. On the three-hour drive there, we were filled with great expectations of catching some great curls. What actually happened when we arrived had the potential to be the greatest tragedy of my life.

We pulled into the parking lot, got our things out of the trunk of our car, and walked toward the beach. As we approached, I noticed an enormous mound of sand about six feet high running the entire length of the beach that wasn't there on any of our previous trips. On top of the mound of sand lay a dead seal. The pounding surf had completely rearranged the landscape. The friendly little cove we'd always known had suddenly changed.

After inspecting the dead seal, my gaze turned to the enormous waves. Neither I nor my kids had ever seen 20-foot waves in person before. We talked about whether we wanted to go in the surf and take a chance on being injured. They opted to stay on the beach where it was safe. My sense of adventure got the best of me, so I pulled my wet suit on and paddled into the surf. I spent the next hour in a slightly terrified state of mind trying to read the waves as they continually grew in size. It was all I could do to hang onto my board and not get beaten to death by the enormous waves.

I was able to catch a few of the smaller ones and ride them for a while, but the water was freezing cold. Even with a good wet suit, I was beginning to shiver. When a large wave approached, I paddled in the direction it was going, but the volume of water was so great that when the curl caught up with me, it drove me forcefully to the bottom. The hydraulic action of the surf held me under and no amount of swimming would bring me up. I had to wait like a pair of pants in a washing machine for the wave to pass so I could come up for air. In one of the waves, I actually thought for a few moments that I might be killed if I stayed out there. As I was under water, I felt like God asked me if the thrill I was having was worth the risk to my life. That was when I realized I'd had enough. Cold and weakened, I managed to swim ashore to safety. As I sat on the beach with my kids the rest of the afternoon, I pondered the awesome power of the sea, knowing I would never see it the same way again.

To the casual observer, there isn't much in this encounter that might be seen as divine revelation. But when God speaks to us through nature, it's often in relation to our circumstances at the time. The things we experience in nature are often similar to the things that are on our mind. I had been thinking a lot about prophecies concerning the coming move of God that had often been represented by a large wave, and here I was having an encounter with a wave bigger than I had ever seen before. The first hint that God wanted to get my attention and speak to me about something specific was the fact that I was personally seeing in nature, something people had been seeing prophetically for many years. I wasn't absolutely certain, but I had a hunch that God wanted to illustrate a few things that day and have me take note of them.

The first impression I had was that the wave—and my relationship to it—was not what I was expecting it to be. I believed we would see some pretty big waves based on the fact that there was a full moon, which has a stronger than normal effect on the tides. I expected that larger waves would mean better surfing, but what it actually meant was more dangerous surfing, and not just dangerous, but potentially deadly surfing.

It was time for me to draw some comparisons. In my mind, I know that people have been looking forward to the changes God has planned for the church. This is because they see a need for wide and sweeping changes. But few have considered the full impact these changes might have. Churches that have built platforms honoring men instead of God may be left in ruins in the coming wave. Spiritually dead churches may likewise be closed for good. When people think of the changes God will bring to the church, they don't generally think in terms of the negative impacts it may have on people's lives, but if the coming wave illustrates the removal of some churches, there will be hardship for many. I wrote many more details in the prophetic word that are not included here. The point is not the prophetic word itself, but how God can speak to us through nature.

CHAPTER THIRTEEN

Circumstances

MANY PEOPLE HAVE RECOGNIZED GOD speaking to them through the circumstances of their lives. Sometimes those circumstances are positive. God arranges meetings and gives us favor with certain people that benefit us and them. In the two volumes of *My Craziest Adventures with God,* I share dozens of stories where God arranged for me to have encounters with strangers for His divine purposes. But some of the circumstances we go through are difficult. In this chapter, I'm going to share with you the most difficult times I've ever experienced, so that when you go through your own times of trial, you'll know how God can speak to you through them.

A few months after meeting Jesus, while sitting beside my wood-burning stove late at night, I had a difficult conversation with God. Through a thought impression that popped into my mind, He asked me how much I loved Him.

"I love you more than anything or anyone," I said.

Through another thought impression, I heard His reply. "What would you be willing to give up for me?"

"Everything," I replied.

"Really?" He asked.

Because I was feeling bold about my love for Him I said, "You can take my wife, take my kids, take my job, and take this house. You can take it all away. Just don't ever leave me." In hindsight, the scene was eerily reminiscent of the conversation Jesus had with Peter before Peter denied him three times.

Not long after our fireside chat, a complaint was filed against me by one of my chiefs. The complaint resulted in a protracted state investigation into several transports that I went on. The investigation led my department to place me on administrative leave without pay, which was a violation of the collective bargaining contract. The violation led to a grievance between the union and the administration that would drag on for over a year, result in numerous hearings, and cost the union and the department thousands of dollars in legal fees.

I had never been unemployed before. And the odd thing was that technically, I still had a job. I just didn't have a paycheck or benefits for 16 months. The department didn't want to pay me, but neither did they want me to collect unemployment so they disputed my unemployment claim. Because I was undergoing a state investigation, no other fire department or ambulance service in the state would consider hiring me. All of this caused me to wonder what God was up to. But I felt as though He was trying in His own way to teach me something about Him and about me that I needed to know. I had only been a believer for a few months and I had much to learn.

I had always been a self-sufficient man. I hated the idea of relying on someone else for financial support. I was a little proud of the fact that I had never been unemployed and never needed to rely on the government or anyone else for my financial provision. But through this particular circumstance of being able to neither earn a paycheck nor collect unemployment, He revealed that He is *Jehovah Jireh,* which means… "the Lord who is my provider" and I learned that I must never again believe that I was the one responsible for my own paycheck.

I was cleared of any wrongdoing during the investigation, but the state had a policy of placing anyone who was investigated on a three-year probation. Eventually, I was fired from my job, but not before a second complaint was filed and another investigation ensued. Once again, I was cleared of any wrongdoing and placed on probation for another three years.

My wife at the time felt as though I must be guilty of the charges against me. She couldn't believe my employer would accuse me of wrongdoing without good cause. She ended up taking the side of those who had accused me, and that caused her to mistrust me. Her mistrust of me destroyed my ability to trust her. It wasn't long before I found a sympathetic female coworker who was willing to take my side. We had an affair and eventually my wife began to suspect something was going on. One day, when we were picking up our kids after school, we got into a loud exchange in the parking lot which drew a crowd of onlookers. Someone in the crowd called the police and I was arrested.

After I was arrested, my wife sought legal counsel and asked for separation. We were eventually divorced. The divorce was probably the most tragic event of my life. We had been together for more than 20 years. I can only imagine that like me, my ex-wife must have gone through an emotional firestorm during the proceedings. She was granted permission by a judge to move 2,000 miles away with our twins who were 13 years old. I had always been very close to my kids, but the affair and divorce caused my daughter to hate me. She refused to return my phone calls. The thought of her not wanting to speak to me broke my heart.

Divorce is hard on everyone involved. In addition to causing emotional hardship, in most cases, it's a financially devastating process that takes years to recover from. Because I was forced to move out and pay rent for another house, in addition to the mortgage for the house we owned, we nearly lost our home to foreclosure. We avoided that, but had to sell it for a lot less than it was worth. We lost our truck and what little money we managed to earn went to legal fees.

Losing things that took years of hard work to acquire was very difficult, but the loss of my kids was *by far* the hardest part of the divorce. My marriage had been going downhill for years. There was very little love left between us. But I loved the twins dearly. Being away from them was one of the most painful things I've ever experienced. Fortunately, my son was willing to keep in touch with me. He was my lifeline during a time of great difficulty. I didn't know when I would see the kids again and I wondered if I had permanently destroyed my relationship with my daughter. I wasn't certain she would ever forgive me. Some days I wondered if I would ever see her again.

During these times, I reflected on my fireside conversation with God. Even though I said He could take these things from me, I had a sense that He was not the one doing it. I had read the book of Job and I knew that it was Satan who afflicted him and tried to ruin his life. I had also read where Jesus said He came to give us an abundant life, but the thief came to steal, kill, and destroy. At the end of Job's trials, God restored and multiplied what the enemy had taken from him. This knowledge gave me hope that one day, everything would be made right again.

Eight months after the twins left, they returned. My daughter and I had a long talk about what had happened. She forgave me and today our relationship is better than it was before the divorce. Not long after the kids returned, I married a wonderful woman who has made my life a joy every day since then. That year we moved into a beautiful home. The job I took after leaving the fire department was the best one I ever had. In short order, God restored everything I had lost.

What the enemy intended for evil, God intended for good. He spoke to me often through these circumstances. He taught me about His faithfulness; I never once sensed that He had abandoned me. He taught me about His wisdom; no one could have imagined how all this devastation would be redeemed. He taught me about His ability to provide for all my needs when my own ability to provide was removed. He taught me many other things, most of which revealed that He is more caring and compassionate than I ever imagined. The truth is—the difficulties that

I faced happened to develop character in me that probably couldn't have been developed any other way. Even though the circumstances I faced were not the direct result of God's actions, the circumstances provided an opportunity for God to teach me because I was willing to learn. So if you're facing difficult events that seem to have no purpose, remember that every hardship we encounter, every struggle we endure, and every victory we experience has the potential to remove from us the things we don't need and develop in us the things we do.

CHAPTER FOURTEEN

Art

IN THIS CHAPTER, I'LL DISCUSS the ways in which God speaks to us through art. I'm married to an artist and only recently began seeing how God speaks through her art. If you've seldom thought about this, I hope this chapter helps you to see that He is speaking to us in ways we sometimes fail to consider.

At the opening of Genesis we see God working as the Creator of the universe. Not only do we see Him create things that serve a purpose, but we also see Him creating things simply because they're "pleasing to the eye." Beauty is the sole reason for some of His creation, and because we are created in His image, we too have the ability and desire to appreciate and create things simply for the aesthetic beauty they provide. This is a key to understanding how God speaks through art. If imagination, creativity, and beauty are important to God, they might also be important to us.

Creativity and the arts are central to God's instructions in Genesis 2:15 to "cultivate the earth." This directive gives us authority not simply to cultivate a garden, but to shape and transform (to cultivate) our culture. We're responsible for influencing the culture around us, which includes art, music, literature, and other creative endeavors, that through them we might reflect God's glory. One of the things we do as ambassadors of God's kingdom is reflect His eternal character and beauty through art.

Art has many different purposes and it might be helpful to first understand what they are. We're going to take a short lesson in art appreciation from C. S. Lewis. This section contains a number of observations from him which were taken from a book he wrote titled, *An Experiment in Criticism* (Cambridge University Press, 1965).

Lewis believed one of the purposes for art is that we have a need for a view of life that transcends our own limited view. When we behold art, in a sense, we are given an opportunity to view life from the viewpoint of others. When asked why people read literature, this was his reply:

> The nearest I have yet got to an answer is that we seek an enlargement of our being. We want to be more than ourselves. Each of us by nature sees the whole world from one point of view with a perspective and a selectiveness peculiar to himself... We want to see with other eyes, to imagine with other imaginations, to feel with other hearts, as well as with our own... We therefore delight to enter into other men's beliefs, even though we think them untrue. And into their passions, though we think them depraved... Literature enlarges our being by admitting us to experiences not our own... My own eyes are not enough for me, I will see through those of others... I will see what others have invented... In reading great literature I become a thousand men and yet remain myself... I see with a thousand eyes, but it is still I who see. Here, as in worship, in love, in moral action, and in knowing, I transcend myself; and am never more myself than when I do.

Getting down to the specific purpose for art Lewis writes:

> The first demand any work of any art makes upon us is surrender. Look. Listen. Receive. Get yourself out of the way (there is no

good asking first whether the work before you deserves such a surrender, for until you have surrendered you cannot possibly find out).

He notes there are two ways in which we can view a work of art. One way is to view it without any expectation at all, except that it has something unique to impart to us. "We sit down before [a work of art] in order to have something done to us, not that we may do things with it." The best way to approach art and literature is to "receive" them. He writes, "When we 'receive' it we exert our senses and imagination and various other powers according to a pattern invented by the artist." Lewis believed there is an inherent message in every work of art and that we must simply allow it to be revealed to us.

The other approach is to view art in order to fill a particular need or to confirm something that already exists in our mind. Lewis says individuals who view it this way "use" art. He writes, "When we 'use' it, we treat it as assistance for our own activities."

For centuries—and particularly during the Renaissance—the church was the greatest patron of the arts. Artists and their art informed the world about the realities of God. During the Protestant reformation, one segment of the church began to take a dim view of art, believing it to be sensual and that it had become an object of worship. The reformers turned their backs on art and many in the Protestant church have had little use for it since. Those who embrace art today do so largely because they see its use as a medium for a message. Rather than enjoying or appreciating art for its aesthetic beauty, we use it like we use blankets and water pitchers—to serve functions that we deem important. Christian thinking about art has suffered from pragmatism. For many Christians, art only has value to the degree that it conveys a religious message. We've turned it into little more than a billboard for a religious worldview. Lewis takes exception to this view of art:

> To use art merely to promote a practical or didactic purpose, even a Christian one, would strip the work of art of any aesthetic qualities it may possess and offer, and reduce it, possibly, to a boring anesthetic. Rather, then, our first response to art was to understand it in the sense of standing *under* it, enjoy it, receive

from it, and experience the experience, know the story, see the colors, taste the realities, and enjoy the pleasures it offered.

Lewis believed that art wasn't meant to promote ideological agendas. Putting a religious message above aesthetic quality leads to art that is not aesthetically pleasing, but boring and trite—defeating one of the main purposes for art. Rather than being glaringly obvious, He believed the message God intends to impart through a work of art "bubbles up" in subtle ways that we often fail to recognize consciously.

Art that carries an overtly religious message can suffer the same problems we might see in commercial or advertising art. When an artist focuses on rendering the right slogan or icon to convey a particular message, their attention is not *primarily* on the elements that make for masterful art. Commercial art is seldom found in museums and galleries—although there are some exceptions. Art that inspires and is aesthetically pleasing is created using criteria that have less to do with the message itself, and more to do with the way in which the work of art is brought together. Allow me to illustrate:

There are rules a writer must follow if they hope to create an essay that brings pleasure to a reader. Proper use of grammar, spelling, rhyme, meter, and punctuation are essential if a writer hopes to convey a meaningful message. While a certain message may be found in a series of words—it is the organization of the words that causes the desired effect upon the soul. In the same way, there are concepts that when used properly, create an aesthetically pleasing work of art. Skilled artists don't create a masterful painting haphazardly. They apply their knowledge of color theory, composition, the use of shadow, highlight, texture, and they employ different brush techniques to create a painting that captures the imagination of a viewer. Art that is aesthetically pleasing can speak to anyone—regardless of their religious view—and God may use such art as a means to deliver His own message.

Art that is created to convey an overtly Christian message is often of low quality. This is why such art is not highly prized by art collectors and museums. If you're a Christian and you believe the secular world rejects Christian art because of its religious motifs, consider that many of the works of the great masters of the Renaissance depicted biblical scenes. This art is highly prized for its quality in spite of its biblical imagery. The secular world will accept Christian art if it is on par with art being produced by master artists.

Christian films have a similar reputation for being of poor quality. Screenplays are often poorly written, acting is often sub-par, and technical production tends to be weak. Poor quality translates to poor acceptance among society. Non-Christians seldom pay money to see films that are overtly Christian in nature and when they do, their reviews are usually negative.

Christian books are not immune to these problems. Very few Christian books are of high enough quality that they can be considered true literature. A notable exception is a pair of books written by Lewis that were described by one of the most respected science fiction writers of all time—Arthur C. Clarke: "Less sympathetic to our aims was Dr. C. S. Lewis, author of two of the very few works of space fiction that can be classed as literature—*Out of the Silent Planet* and *Perelandra.*"

Although Lewis disagreed with the ideas put forth by Clarke and other science fiction writers of the day, his work was highly regarded by his contemporaries. Clarke noted that Lewis' books were among the few that could truly be called literature. This remark was made because Clarke recognized their exceptional quality. Lewis believed Christians must first be good at the technical aspects of what they do. Rather than create poor quality art that was saturated with religion, Lewis believed the best strategy was to create excellent quality art and literature that contained subtle messages. To that end, He wrote *The Chronicles of Narnia.*

Until J. K. Rowling penned the *Harry Potter* series, Lewis's Narnia books were the best-selling children's fantasy books of all time. Their popularity was due to the fact that Lewis was an exceptionally skilled writer. Rather than using an overtly Christian message, *The Chronicles of Narnia* tell a tale of redemption clothed in classic fictional fantasy. Lewis believed art and literature have the potential to reach the far recesses of the human imagination in ways a Sunday sermon cannot. He illustrated this idea in his article, "Sometimes Fairy Stories May Say Best What's to Be Said:"

Why did one find it so hard to feel as one was told one ought to feel about God or about the sufferings of Christ? I thought the chief reason was that one was told one ought to. An obligation to feel can freeze feeling. But suppose by casting all these things into an imaginary world, stripping them of their stained-glass and Sunday School associations, one could make them for the first time appear in their real potency. Could one not thus steal past those watchful dragons? I thought one could.

Lewis believed a generation of readers could be taught the realities of God's kingdom if he first wrote children's stories the way they ought to be written. As with the parables Jesus told, the realities of the kingdom would be hidden, except to those who had "eyes to see" them. Although many did not realize it at the time, as they read the Narnia books, they were being taught about God's plan of redemption.

Being a writer, I gravitate toward gifted writers. I draw inspiration from them, pick up tips and learn from their examples. We all need role models and over the years, Lewis has become the main person by whom I gauge my own writing. While writing, I often wonder to myself, how would Lewis have addressed this issue? How would he build this argument? Which words might he choose to convey this idea?

I never had a chance to meet Lewis. He died in 1963. One day, I spent several hours wondering about him and reflecting on how his life has impacted mine. Time itself seemed to stand still that afternoon, and then I went to sleep. That night I had a dream where Lewis paid me a visit. The purpose of our meeting was so that he might teach me a few things about writing. I didn't see him in the way you might typically see someone in a dream. It's not as though we were sitting at a table talking. I simply "knew" I was in his presence, the way you know certain facts in a dream. I didn't hear him speak the way you might hear someone speak in a dream. He spoke to me spirit-to-spirit through the transmission of thoughts.

In the dream, I was being tutored by the spirit of one of my favorite men and what he had to say surprised me. He didn't teach me about drawing closer to God or about being a better Christian. If what I needed was another sermon he could have given me one. Instead, he told me about how the proper selection of words was critical to being a successful writer and illustrated his point with several stories about the problems he ran into by not choosing the right words. He noted that our choice of words creates either a favorable or an unfavorable experience in the mind of a reader and that the selection of one word or another can make a huge difference in how our writing is perceived. He gave several examples of how the choice of this word or that one created a completely different set of circumstances and told me to choose my words with care. That is a brief summary of the dream.

True to his convictions while he was walking the earth, Lewis imparted to me something he believed at the core of his soul: The world doesn't need more Christians who write about Christianity in a mediocre way. What the world needs is more skilled writers who write well about all the issues of life, and who *happen* to be Christians. Art, music, and literature that is of the highest quality has a chance to be seen by the largest audience. The success of Lewis' books is evidence of that. Paintings, literature, and music that are of high quality—even though their message is subtle—can touch people in a powerful way.

I once heard a testimony about how a painting changed someone's life forever. It's the story of an agnostic woman who visited a secular art gallery. The woman viewed one painting after another then found herself drawn to one painting in particular. She stood in front of it for a long time—her mouth hanging open in shock as tears flowed down her cheeks. A friend noticed and asked what was wrong with her. She replied that she had never seen anything so beautiful as the painting that hung in front of her. "I never believed in God," she confessed. "But I now know that God must exist. For only the mind of an incredibly talented and brilliant God could inspire someone to create a painting such as this." Without anything that overtly spoke of Christianity, one woman's agnosticism was turned to belief in God.

My wife is trained as an oil painter in the style of the old masters. She has also worked in the field of advertising and commercial art. Being an artist is part of her divine calling. As I'm writing this chapter she's taking classes to sharpen her skills in drawing and painting. She's got a lot of talent already, but she feels compelled to move up to a new level. Her aim is to continually improve her skills to create paintings that are every bit as good from a technical standpoint, as those that hang in galleries and museums.

She's learning the lesson that Lewis preached. In fact, she was the first person to show me what that lesson looks like in practice. My wife used to wonder how God would speak to others through her art if she didn't want to paint the standard motifs of Christianity—wooden crosses, lions, lambs, or Jesus. But God is showing her that it is perfectly alright to paint landscapes, portraits, and abstract forms. In some of her paintings (if you can receive what is there) you'll find subtle suggestions of the cross, hints of the heavens, or titles that subtly speak of God. The average person may not see any of it, but those who have eyes to see will notice these things, even if only subconsciously, and they will be drawn to God through them. She's learning that it's not up to her to devise a clever or emotionally appealing message. It is God who is able to reach virtually anyone at any time with a message just for them. Jesus said no one comes to Him unless they are drawn by the Father. How God speaks to each person through a work of art is dependent on His knowledge of when and how they can best be drawn into that relationship.

As Lewis said, perhaps we could strip the art of its "stained-glass and Sunday School associations." I wonder what impact our art would have on the world if we would become highly proficient in our artistic skills and let God elevate His message from the work we produce.

CHAPTER FIFTEEN

Film

ONE OF THE MOST POPULAR films of all time is the science fiction classic *The Matrix*. This film is not overtly Christian, yet many people —believers and non-believers alike—have found illustrations buried in it that speak of God and His kingdom. *The Matrix* depicts a dark future-world where reality, as it is perceived by most humans, is a simulated world known as "the Matrix."

The Matrix is a cyber-world created by intelligent machines who subdue humans so they can harness their body heat and electrical energy to use them as a power source. Laurence Fishburne plays Morpheus, a prophet who is alerted to the advent of a savior whose destiny is to free the world from the bondage of the Matrix. Keanu Reeves plays Neo, a computer programmer who learns the truth about the Matrix and is drawn into a bizarre series of events which bring about the defeat of the film's cyber-villains.

Morpheus and Neo are cast in roles so reminiscent of John the Baptist and Jesus that when I first saw the film, (before I was a Christian) I immediately recognized the connection between them and their biblical counterparts. The way in which the battle between good and evil is portrayed in the film began to soften my naturalistic way of thinking. I wonder to this day how much influence the film had on me on a subconscious level, as a little more than a year after seeing the film, I became a Christian.

The Matrix was well-received by critics, winning four Academy Awards. It received high praise for its innovative visual effects and cinematography. Like *The Chronicles of Narnia*, *The Matrix* was a big success because it was well-executed. It did exactly what films are supposed to do. And it moved viewers to consider biblical realities because it had hidden spiritual themes they couldn't help but notice. While *The Matrix* doesn't have a message as tangibly spiritual as films like *Heaven is for Real*, or *The Passion of the Christ*, because of its broad appeal, it has the potential to impact more people than any Christian film ever made.

Early in 2015, I took a job working as a paramedic in Phoenix, Arizona. Shortly after I was hired, I had a dream where I was given a pass by my employer that granted me free access to movie theaters. All I had to do was show the pass at the door and I'd be allowed into a theater without paying. The pass was a benefit of working for my new employer. In the dream, my coworkers and I were being taught how to use this benefit without abusing it.

Around the same time I had the dream, my EMT partner and I were having a slow shift and we were hanging out with another crew at a shopping mall. One of the EMTs got the bright idea to go into the theater and ask if we could watch a movie on duty. He returned and told us we could go in for free. *American Sniper* happened to be playing, so we went inside and took a seat.

Although the film is filled with profanity, killing, and other things which Christians might find objectionable, as I watched the film, God brought to mind one dream after another He had given me over the previous eight years. The dreams all depicted military themes. Many of them were dreams I had never fully understood. Over the next month, the Holy Spirit connected scenes from the film to the dreams He had given me and I began seeing spiritual principles emerge. He taught me that there are a lot of parallels between the military actions of Navy SEALS and the kind of warfare believers wage against the kingdom of darkness. This is another case of a well-made film that lacked an overtly religious message, but which nonetheless taught me about the spiritual realities of the kingdom.

The Christian film industry has many zealous men and women who are eager to spread the gospel, but who lack the kind of skill, budgets, and imagination necessary to produce high-quality films. Instead, they often end up producing celluloid sermons that only appeal to those who are already Christians. The result of their efforts is that the church ends up evangelizing itself. Before a movie can teach the world anything about God, it must first be what films are meant to be: well-written and well-acted stories that enlighten, engage, reveal beauty, entertain, and capture our imaginations. When film makers fail to do this, the result is Christian art that puts the world to sleep. But if they make films the way they are intended to be made, society can be transformed by them.

CHAPTER SIXTEEN

Music

THE CELEBRATED FRENCH AUTHOR VICTOR Hugo once said, "Music expresses that which cannot be put into words and that which cannot remain silent."

God frequently speaks to me through music. I've often been touched by the lyrics of a song as they spoke almost prophetically, to some pressing issue I had been dealing with. After I met my second wife, we went through a class together where one of the goals was to uncover a lie we had believed most of our life. My wife's lie happened to be "You don't love me." She had for some reason, always seen herself as unlovable. Although many people said they loved her, deep down inside, she never felt as if they were being honest. She truly believed no one could really love her. I can only imagine how hard it must have been living with such a lie her entire life. She happened to marry me and it's been my greatest pleasure each day to do two or three things to prove to her that it really was a lie and that she truly is lovable. We both enjoy many types of music. And we've both developed a love for some of the music from our parent's generation. Frank Sinatra is a particular favorite. My wife used to be a vocalist and she still loves to sing. There are several songs performed by Sinatra that when we hear them, touch us deeply. Sometimes we sing along together to "The Way You Look Tonight" and God uses it to reaffirm to her that she is lovely to me.

The lie that I believed was "You don't understand me." Since I was a child, I've never felt that anyone has truly understood me. I spent time and energy trying to make myself understood to my friends and family but no matter how I tried, the real me was never something anyone could grasp. Introverts prefer to keep to themselves, but I'm an extrovert by nature. So my life's ambition has been to share the deepest parts of my soul with anyone who might try to understand me. Perhaps that's one reason I'm drawn to writing. It provides an outlet for my need to be understood. For years, whenever I heard the song "Don't Let Me Be Misunderstood" a popular tune from the 1960s, I felt as if God was using the song to speak to me about my private pain. Fortunately, my wife finds me quite easy to understand. To her—there is little mystery about me. What amazes me most is that in the same way God loves me just as I am, after she came to understand me, she was still able to love me, unconditionally.

I have a friend named Todd Adams, who is a percussionist. He's been hearing God speak through music for decades. Todd is part of a worship band but the kind of music the band plays is like nothing I've ever heard. They don't play hymns or even what can be referred to as "songs" with lyrics. Elizabeth Cooper is the band's leader. She plays keyboard and guitar. Her husband Daniel plays drums. Todd plays everything from wind chimes and flute to djembe and occasionally employs an aboriginal form of throat singing that's impossible to describe. I had an opportunity to spend a weekend with the band at a speaking engagement I did for a group of friends. Todd's goal with his percussion is to hear the sounds that are coming from heaven and play them to the best of his ability. The rhythms he hears are seldom the same and they're subject to change at any time. Sometimes what he hears can only be described as the heartbeat of God. He senses the beat and plays it on his drum. He senses other sounds in the heavens and adds them as they are heard. The sounds he hears coming from heaven are very diverse, which is why he sits in a cage lined with a vast array of odd instruments that he's collected over the years. Each instrument emits a sound similar to one he hears coming from heaven.

Elizabeth also listens for the sounds she hears coming from heaven. Whatever melodies and rhythms she hears—she plays. She also hears the voice of the Holy Spirit and sings whatever she hears Him speaking. The messages she sings can be about almost anything. For this reason, there are no lyrics to help the audience sing along. But those who are able to sense the same sounds in the spirit often join in.

The weekend I was with the band, there happened to be many people in the audience who suffered from conditions such as dissociative identity disorder and bi-polar disorder. During the first session, the percussion seemed to create an atmosphere that attracted angels and I sensed an increasing angelic presence in the room throughout the evening. Elizabeth began making declarations about freedom from emotional bondage and about things from the past that were holding people back. I watched as about half the audience went to the floor and over the next 90 minutes, the Holy Spirit took many of my friends through a process of emotional healing.

Todd drives a public transit bus for those with physical handicaps. As a way to help fund his mission trips, he recorded a couple of CDs. One day he played a track from one of his CDs on his bus route and asked one of the riders to listen to it. Todd had originally composed it as a song of mourning for the death of a dear friend. The bus rider loved the music so much he bought the CD. Months later, he confessed that the medications he was taking didn't relieve his chronic pain but when he played the track, it somehow eased his pain. Todd's music became part of his regimen for pain management.

Here is another way in which God speaks through music:

Millions of people over the last few centuries have heard of Johann Sebastian Bach. Yet in his day, Bach was virtually unknown outside of the German towns where he quietly lived and worked. Bach never sought fame or fortune. He was employed for most of his career by small churches and lived in relative obscurity. Bach said, "Music's only purpose should be the glory of God and the recreation of the human spirit." Music, according to Bach, was given to glorify God and to edify us. You would have to look hard to find anyone who gave more joy to the world than Bach. More than 250 years after his death, Bach's music still lifts the heart and energizes the soul.

Bach's influence on cultures around the world has been impressive, particularly in Japan where less than one percent of the population are Christians. The beauty of Bach's music and gospel-centered lyrics have created a spiritual awakening where Japanese citizens are exploring the person of Jesus. Christianity has never been widely embraced by the people of Japan. In the 18th century, European traders and missionaries came to the island and had mixed success; commerce did well, but the gospel was largely rejected. But Japan embraced the music of Western culture and in particular—the music of Bach. His popularity is so great today that classes at the Felix Mendolssohn Academy in Bach's hometown of Leipzig, Germany are filled with Japanese students. These students are learning about more than just Bach's music. They're learning about the Spirit of God that moved him to write.

A Japanese Christian conductor named Masaaki Suzuki said:

"Bach works as a missionary among our people. After each concert, people crowd the podium wishing to talk to me about topics that are normally taboo in our society—death, for example. Then they inevitably ask me what 'hope' means to Christians. I believe that Bach has already converted tens of thousands of Japanese to the Christian faith. A Japanese musicologist named Keisuke traveled all the way to Bach's home church in Germany to study the biblical basis for Bach's cantatas. He ended up seeking out a pastor and asking, 'It is not enough to read Christian texts. I want to be a Christian myself. Please baptize me.' Another Japanese musician, a female organist and former Buddhist named Yoko, said, 'Bach introduced me to God, Jesus, and Christianity. When I play a fugue, I can hear Bach talking to God.'"

CHAPTER SEVENTEEN

Emotions

IN MY WORK, I FREQUENTLY transport people who are addicted to drugs and alcohol. Many of these people are homeless. I'd like to say that I have a heart full of compassion and love for them. But if I said that, I would be lying. To be honest, I don't have a lot of natural affection for these people. I've been on the receiving end of my share of violence and abuse from some of my former patients who were struggling with addiction. Yet God in His wisdom gave me a calling to minister healing to these folks. One of the most frequent ways He communicates to me about an addicted person He wants me to pray with is through my emotions.

I've sat in the back of the ambulance a thousand times writing my report as I transported an intoxicated, verbally abusive person to the hospital. I generally try to remain as uninvolved with them as I can. The more detached I remain, the less likelihood there is of an altercation.

But I've been surprised at how often I've felt a deep ache in my soul over the condition of one of these people. There I am, minding my own business, writing my report, when a wave of broken-heartedness comes over me. At first I didn't understand what was happening when I felt these emotions. I'm sure I shrugged them off a number of times and didn't respond the way I should have. But gradually, I began seeing a pattern in these emotions and one day, when I was feeling the deep broken-heartedness over a drunk I'd just met, I asked if I could pray for him. He smiled and said, "I'd love that."

One of the most reliable ways of knowing you're sensing something from God is knowing it didn't come from you. I suspect the problem some of us have is that we aren't sure which emotions are ours, and which are external to us. We've been trained to think that every emotion we feel is one of our own emotions. But emotions are tricky things. Demons can make us feel certain emotions, and so can angels. And God often conveys to us His emotions when He wants to communicate something to us. Even though these emotions *seem* to be ours—because they feel the same as the rest of our emotions—there are subtle clues that point to an external origin for some of them.

I think we probably give ourselves more credit for having compassion and love for others than we rightly deserve. It's feels good to give ourselves a pat on the back when we show unusual kindness to a stranger. It's human nature to think we're the one responsible for "paying it forward" or helping someone. But I suspect that in many cases, what's happening is that God is communicating the way He feels toward that stranger through our emotions. After we sense His heart for them, we're moved to do the right thing—something other than what we would normally do. We take the credit for our good deed, but in many cases, God was behind it all. Most of us feel God's emotions for the people around us more often than we realize, but we're simply not aware of where the emotions are coming from.

Unless you know yourself well, it can be difficult to determine which emotions are "yours" and which are "not yours." I've had many conversations with people who suddenly realized the unusual feelings of depression and hopelessness they experienced were not coming from them. They were coming from God and they were intended to make them aware that a friend was struggling with depression and God wanted them to pray for their friend.

In the same way that God can give us a sudden sensation of pain in our knee as a word of knowledge for the knee pain of someone else, which He wants to heal, He can give us emotions that are not ours. They're from Him and they're intended to let us know that someone near us is feeling those same emotions and needs prayer.

I have friends who cannot walk into a crowded room without feeling the anger, anxiety, jealousy, fear, and all the other emotions that are being felt by people in the room. These individuals have a heightened awareness of how others feel. They're sometimes referred to as "empaths" because of their ability to easily sense and empathize with how others feel. Extreme empathy might seem like a gift that only certain people are born with, but like all other spiritual abilities, empathy is an innate ability we all possess. Anyone is able to sense the emotions of another person. Rather than being a special gift, what these people have is a highly-developed ability that is common to us all. Just as with any other spiritual ability, we can learn to become more sensitive to the feelings of others with practice.

I also know some believers who sense feelings of oppression, hopelessness, fear, and other emotions when they drive through certain towns. They've learned that the emotions they feel are being sent from God and are intended to lead them to pray for the people of that town. These divine emotions can be thought of as a kind of prophetic burden that God gives people to move them to pray. They pray as they're led by the emotions they feel, and they keep praying until the emotions are gone.

The Prince of Peace

Another way to deal with the human emotions God reveals is to change the emotions others are presently experiencing. During the writing of this book, I had a dream featuring a man who was filled with peace. He happened to be around people who didn't have much peace. In the dream, the emotions of people were symbolized by boards covered with fabric.

The peace-filled man was able to give others the peace that he had. When he wanted to do this, he pulled out a spray can and sprayed over the fabric on someone's emotional board. Then he cut a piece of fabric from his own emotional board and pasted it on the board of the other person and in doing so—he gave them his peace.

One of the implications of seeing Jesus as a flesh and blood role model (and not merely as our savior) is that we can do the things He did and live the way He lived. This is the practical side of being His disciple. He said to His disciples, "Peace I leave with you, My peace I give to you," (see Jn. 14:27). He transferred His own peace to those who didn't have it. And we can learn to do the same. We can learn to impart peace to those who are filled with fear, anxiety, and worry. Here's what that might look like:

One day I transported a young man who was having chest pain. He was so afraid he was having a heart attack he didn't tell the nurse who was taking care of him. He also denied it when I asked him, but his wife confronted him about it. "Why don't you tell him about the chest pain?" She asked.

He was afraid. He wasn't sure what would happen if he told us he was having chest pain. In his mind, He was too young for a heart attack and the possibility of cardiac surgery. After we began transporting him to the hospital, I took a seat next to him.

"Hey, Alfred, I have a question for you... would you like me to pray with you?"

He agreed to let me pray for him. Alfred had been under a lot of stress lately—much more than he was used to. The chest pain only made things worse. He also had a severe headache. I asked how bad his headache was. He rated it at eight out of ten in severity.

I placed my hand gently on his shoulder. "Spirit of pain, I command you to leave. Holy Spirit, touch him with your power and remove all sickness and pain from him. I bless your work of healing and Lord, I thank you for your mercy." I prayed for a few more minutes and asked what he felt.

"It's gone. It's all gone."

"Your headache?"

"Yeah."

"Are you lying to me?"

"No, I'm not lying. As soon as you put your hand on me and started praying, it left. It was like... two seconds later."

We both smiled and laughed and started talking about how amazing God is. Not only was his headache gone, but so was all of his anxiety and fear. "All I feel now is peace," he said with a smile.

I've noticed that many times when I pray for people to be healed, the thing they notice first is that their fear and anxiety disappear and they're overcome by a strong sense of peace. Even if they don't receive physical healing, a majority of them report feeling great peace. I believe that's because Jesus lives in us, and because He is the Prince of Peace, He leaves His calling card wherever He goes and it's felt by the people we encounter.

Of course, a prerequisite for releasing peace to others is having peace in your own life. We can't give to others what we don't have. So if you're lacking the peace of God, you might ask Him to give you His peace so that you can release it to those who need it.

Exercise

If you're sensitive to the emotions of others, it can help to take an inventory of how you're feeling before entering a room or building. If you're happy before going into a room full of people, but after being in the room for a few minutes you begin to feel emotions that were not present earlier—the emotions may not be your own. You might ask God if He's saying anything through the emotions you're feeling. If you believe you're feeling an emotion that isn't yours, you might ask God what the emotion means and who it is for. Ask Him if there is someone in the room who needs prayer and if you receive confirmation about someone, ask them if they would like prayer.

Notes

CHAPTER EIGHTEEN

Angels

GOD CAN SPEAK TO US directly, and He often does just that through His Spirit. But many times, He chooses to speak to us through His messengers instead. Along with learning to hear the voice of God, we can learn how to hear angels when they deliver messages. Angels are sent by God to all of mankind to assist us along our path of life. Both Christians and non-Christians have angels who watch over and assist them. The purpose of this chapter is to encourage you to learn how to hear the messages they bring so that you might fulfill your heavenly assignments and grow in your knowledge of God and His kingdom.

One of the most common ways angels appear as recorded in the Bible are as messengers who impart instruction or news to people in dreams. In Genesis chapter 31, an angel of the Lord appeared to Jacob in a dream. It contained a symbolic message, which the angel interpreted for him—it was time for Jacob to return to his father's home (see Gen. 31:11-13).

When Abraham sent his servant to find a wife for his son Isaac, an angel was sent with him to help prosper the servant during his journey (see Gen. 24:40).

An angel gave Abraham's wife Hagar a message that her son, Ishmael, would not die of thirst in the wilderness, but that God had heard his cries and provided a pool of water for them (see Gen. 21:17-19).

An angel appeared to Manoah's wife to announce the birth of her child Samson. The Angel gave her strict instructions about what to do in preparation for his birth. It was also revealed that her son would take the vow of a Nazarite, and that he would deliver his people from the Philistines (see Judges 13:2-5).

An angel appeared to Elijah after he had called down fire from heaven to consume the armies of his enemies on two occasions. When a third captain approached and begged Elijah not to kill him, the angel instructed Elijah to go with the captain (see 2 Kgs. 1:15).

An angel offered encouragement to the apostle Paul in the midst of a disaster at sea, telling him that all those who sailed with him would not perish in the storm, but that the ship would run aground and they would be saved from death (see Acts 27:23-24).

According to the writer of the book of Hebrews, angels have been sent for the express purpose of ministering to those who will inherit salvation (see Heb. 1:14). Since Christians are the heirs of salvation, angels are sent for the purpose of ministering to us.

As we can see, angels often serve as divine messengers. In fact, the Greek word for angel, *aggelos*, means *messenger*. But not all of the spirits who serve God are messengers. There are a diversity of heavenly spirits with various assignments. Some of these spirits are messengers, but some are ordained for other things. Some heavenly spirits are commissioned to bring healing, such as the one who stood at the pool of Bethesda and stirred the water so that the sick could be healed (see Jn. 5:4). Some specialize in worship such as the living creatures mentioned in the book of Revelation who cried holy, holy, holy, day and night. Some angels are in charge of the weather such as the spirits who held back the wind so that it would not blow on the earth (see Rev. 7:1). Like humans, heavenly spirits are not all alike. They are each a little different and their differences enable them to serve different purposes and carry out different assignments.

I often have indirect communication with angels while praying for people to be healed. Since one of my major assignments from God is healing, I assume I have a number of healing angels assigned to me, though I seldom see them. I usually close my eyes as I'm sitting in my chair praying for someone. As I pray, I see faint images in my mind's eye suggestive of spiritual beings that are moving about in the spirit world. I've given them commands to release healing on the people I'm praying for. To be perfectly honest, I don't know with certainty what effect this has, since I don't have a foolproof way to verify the results, though I have had a number of reliable healing testimonies from people I've prayed with over long distances.

My wife and I most often have direct communication with angels as they deliver messages in the middle of the night. These messages usually come in the form of a voice that we hear speaking, usually in a dream or vision. Our children have also received messages from angels, usually at night. The messages are typically short. They can have an obvious meaning or they may be somewhat cryptic.

At times, a message from an angel will sound like an audible voice. But more often, we have conversations with them the same way we do with the Holy Spirit—through faint thought impressions in our mind. Remember, angels are spirits, just like the Holy Spirit and like our own spirit. Spirit-to-spirit communication is generally carried out the same way, regardless of whether we're hearing from an evil spirit, one of God's angels, or the Holy Spirit. The key to learning how to hear angels is exercising our spiritual senses.

Exercise

Since many of the angelic encounters in the Bible involved dreams, before you go to sleep, ask God to send you an angel with a message. Whatever experience you have that night, write in down. If you receive a cryptic or symbolic message in a dream, ask the Holy Spirit to help you understand it.

Notes

Notes

CHAPTER NINETEEN

Face-to-Face

JESUS IS MAKING A HABIT of visiting my wife on her birthday. So far, the visitations have come through her dreams. For years she had been struggling with the burden of deciding what steps to take next in her career. Although she had been trained as a painter and her heart's desire was to create fine art that flowed from her imagination, she was working as a graphic designer for the past 15 years because it paid the bills. The design work was no longer inspiring her as it once did and it often left her with neck pain and a headache at the end of the day, but she felt afraid of making the changes that would allow her to become a full-time painter. Part of the struggle was that she wasn't certain what God *wanted* her to do. She wondered—if she made the career change, would God bless that decision, or would she fail, leaving us in a difficult place, financially. There was also some anxiety and regret that she had waited too long—that she probably should have done it years ago. It would be almost like starting over.

On her birthday in 2014, she had a dream where Jesus paid her a visit. In the dream, He came to her rather excitedly and handed her a piece of paper. The paper was blank except for the letterhead at the top that appeared in a beautiful pink font which read: "Super Praying Medic's Wife." After handing her the blank piece of paper, He looked excitedly into her eyes and asked, "What are you going to *be*?"

This dream changed the way in which my wife saw her relationship with Jesus. Rather than thinking she had to somehow know what He wanted her to do (and suffer the consequences if she was wrong) she realized that He was actually her biggest fan, and that regardless of which choice she made, He supported her decision. Jesus gave her the sense that she could write whatever she wanted on the blank canvas of her life, so to speak. The dream destroyed some bad theology she had picked up and replaced it with a more accurate portrait of God.

On her birthday in 2015, Jesus paid her another visit in a dream. This is her account:

> I had another dream on my birthday this year. I was sitting (at an easel, I think) painting. There was a wall in front of me as well. Suddenly something red, like blood or paint, began splattering on the right side of the wall in front of me. It started dripping, running quickly down the wall. I wondered if it was coming from a leak in the ceiling. I looked up, straining to see, but couldn't see any evidence of a leak.
>
> With a horizontal motion, I smeared my hand from left to right through the drips, trying to keep them from running all the way down to the floor. Then I looked up again to my left. On the wall, was a large, fabulous, freshly painted portrait of Jesus' face. In the dream, I somehow knew that He painted it Himself—it was a self-portrait painted using only the color red. The portrait was very large and expressive with wild brush strokes, spatters, and drips. To me it was just beautiful!
>
> In the dream, I felt so excited that He painted it—but mostly that He let me see it. I hurried to tell my husband and some other friends in the dream.
>
> Looking back, it all makes sense to me. The red splatters on the wall in the beginning of the dream were coming from the wild brush strokes of Jesus

himself. The paint was flying. He is an artist, a creator of beauty, and He does it with passion!

This visit from Jesus helped confirm that my wife's interest in painting was divinely ordained and perhaps there is even the suggestion that Jesus is so interested in art that He's painting beside her. From the testimonies I've heard where Jesus has visited people in person, His visits seem to be for the purpose of helping us understand our true identity and our divine destiny. One of the most important things you'll ever do is discover your divine destiny. Although there are general purposes for which man was created, there are also unique reasons why each of us is brought into the world. Your divine destiny is the unique set of purposes for which God has created you.

We were created for God's good pleasure. Part of His pleasure is watching us grow into what He designed us to be and to do. How do we know what God has created us for? Your specific destiny is closely tied to the passions of your heart—the things you desire more than anything else. God is the one who gives us these desires and they're given to motivate and propel us toward our divinely ordained destiny. However, many times we let obstacles like time and money prevent us from fully pursuing it. One person's destiny might involve being a painter, but if they believe painting won't pay the bills, they may forego their destiny and instead, settle for a job at a bank. Another person's destiny might be to record music, but if they feel they can't earn a living as a musician, they might settle for a job in a factory. We must learn to trust that if we pursue our destiny, God will provide the time, resources and connections to make us successful.

Exercise #1

Jesus is willing to personally show you what your divine destiny is. It's up to you to ask Him for those details. Ask Him to come to you personally and reveal to you how He sees you and what He created you for. He may appear to you in a number of ways. It may be in a dream or a vision, or it may be that He visits you in what appears to be bodily form. However He reveals Himself, write down what He tells you and believe what He says. Begin to pursue the destiny He reveals to you.

Exercise #2

Fear is what usually prevents us from pursuing our destiny, and the thing that empowers fear is our belief in the lie that we can't earn a living from it.

To remove fear from the equation, ask yourself what you would do if time and money were no object. If you had all the resources you needed, and all the time in the world, what would you do with the rest of your life?

If you're going to live out the destiny God has planned for you, consider taking an inventory of your passions and ask yourself what one thing really gets you excited. It's likely that this one thing is somehow tied to your divine destiny. If there's some career you can name that involves this passion, consider pursuing it and see if God doesn't open a few doors for you.

Notes

What to Do with What You Hear

CHAPTER TWENTY

The Gift of Tongues

NOW THAT WE'VE SURVEYED THE different ways in which God speaks, it's time to look at what we might do with the revelation we receive. In this section, Part Three, we'll discuss the ways in which God speaks to us and through us via the gifts of the Holy Spirit. The gifts of the Holy Spirit are covered in some detail in first Corinthians chapters 12 through 14. If you're not acquainted with these chapters you might read them to become more familiar with the ways in which these gifts are used.

One of the most controversial spiritual gifts mentioned in the New Testament is the gift of speaking in tongues. Although many good people have rejected the idea that God speaks to and through us in this way, I've found that there is great benefit to those who practice this gift. To settle any concerns readers may have, it might be helpful to look at what Jesus said about speaking in tongues. His only mention of speaking in tongues happens to be part of "the great commission" which is accepted by most Christians as His final instructions to His disciples before He ascended into heaven. Here are his words:

> *"And these signs will accompany those who believe: In my name they will drive out demons; they will speak in new tongues."*
> MARK 16:17

Jesus said that speaking in tongues is a supernatural sign that can and should be practiced by His disciples.

When we speak in tongues we may either speak in a language that is known to man or in a heavenly language that is unknown to us. Paul wrote:

> *"Though I speak with the tongues of men and of angels..."*
> 1 COR. 13:1

The language we speak when we operate in this gift allows us to communicate directly with God. The Holy Spirit enables us to speak a language (or several of them) without ever having to learn them. This is why speaking in tongues is considered a gift and not an ability—we receive a divine enabling to do what we could not do otherwise.

Researchers at the University of Pennsylvania recorded scans of the brains of people while they spoke in tongues. The study was published in *The New York Times*. Dr. Andrew Newberg, who headed the study, concluded:

> We noticed a number of changes that occurred functionally in the brain. Our finding of decreased activity in the frontal lobes during the practice of speaking in tongues is fascinating because these subjects truly believe that the spirit of God is moving through them and controlling them to speak... Our brain-imaging research shows us that these subjects are not in control of the usual language centers during this activity, which is consistent with their description of a lack of intentional control while speaking in tongues.

When the participants spoke in tongues, their frontal lobes (the part of the brain that controls voluntary action) showed very little activity. The language center of the brain likewise showed little activity as compared to when the participants spoke normally. As the participants spoke in tongues, researchers were unable to pinpoint which part of the brain was controlling their speech. Dr. Newberg went on to say, "The amazing thing was how the images supported people's interpretation of what was happening. The way they describe it, and what they believe, is that God is talking through them." If there is any doubt that speaking in tongues is a real supernatural phenomenon, this research seems to suggest that it is.

Some leaders teach that the gift of tongues is only for certain people. The Bible teaches otherwise. On the day of Pentecost, when the disciples were filled with the Holy Spirit, everyone in attendance spoke in tongues:

"All of them were filled with the Holy Spirit and began to speak in other tongues as the Spirit enabled them."
ACTS 2:4

The gift of tongues is not only for a select few. Paul said that he wanted every believer to speak in tongues and prophesy:

"I wish you all spoke with tongues, but even more that you prophesied"
1 COR. 14:5

The Bible says that those who speak in tongues are (generally) speaking directly to God:

"For anyone who speaks in a tongue does not speak to men but to God. Indeed, no one understands him; he utters mysteries with his spirit."
1 COR. 14:2

One of the exceptions is when we speak in tongues to declare the wonders of God to others:

"We hear them declaring the wonders of God in our own tongues!"
ACTS 2:11

Or when praising God:

"For they heard them speaking in tongues and praising God."
ACTS 10:46

Those who are experienced with speaking in tongues report that their spirit is strengthened the more they pray in tongues. It also seems to open up a clearer channel of communication between them and God. The gift of speaking in tongues is the one gift given to edify (strengthen) the individual. The rest of the gifts of the Holy Spirit are given to strengthen the body of Christ:

"He who speaks in a tongue edifies himself, but he who prophesies edifies the church."
1 COR. 14:4

When I pray with people for healing or deliverance, my wife often prays alongside me. I begin by praying in English as I'm led by the Spirit—most often through visions. She rarely prays in her native language, which is English, but prays as she is led by the Spirit in tongues. She's become so accustomed to praying in tongues that today it's easier for her to pray in tongues than it is to pray in English.

Occasionally someone will pray in tongues and an interpretation will be given, but not always. When an interpretation is given of something that was said in tongues, it is usually a word of encouragement to an individual or group. In that respect, the interpretation of tongues is similar to the gift of prophecy.

The gift of speaking in tongues is like any other gift. The more we exercise it, the more proficient we'll become at it. If you desire to operate in the gift of tongues, pray for it and believe that you will receive it. Speaking in tongues is not something the Holy Spirit does *to* you. It is rather, a way that He operates *through* you as you speak or pray. The key is that *you* must initiate the process.

When I first began speaking in tongues, I heard in my mind words that were softly spoken in a language I had never heard before. As I've said in other chapters, one way in which you can know revelation is from God is when it sounds unlike anything you would normally think. The words I heard in my mind were completely foreign to me. I assumed they were the words the Holy Spirit wanted me to speak, so I said them to the best of my ability. I have a friend who said the first time he spoke in tongues was when he was riding his motorcycle. His motorcycle was hit by a car and he went flying through the air. He said as soon as he was airborne, he began speaking in tongues.

The apostle Paul said that the main problem with speaking in tongues is that our natural mind doesn't understand what we say:

> *"For if I pray in a tongue, my spirit prays, but my understanding is unfruitful."*
> 1 COR. 14:14

There are times when it isn't necessary to know what we are praying. Paul discussed this in the eighth chapter of Romans:

> *"Likewise the Spirit also helps in our weaknesses. For we do not know what we should pray for as we ought, but the Spirit Himself makes intercession for us with groanings which cannot be uttered. Now He who searches the hearts knows what the mind of the Spirit is, because He makes intercession for the saints according to the will of God."*
> ROM. 8:26-27

Praying in tongues is a way in which the Spirit of God can inspire our prayer when we aren't sure how we ought to pray. The Holy Spirit is our helper, our comforter, our intercessor, and faithful friend. Praying in tongues empowers us when we are weak, comforts us when we are sad, and through it, He intercedes for us according to His perfect will.

Exercise

The gift of speaking in tongues can be activated in just about any way that you can imagine. The process may be a little different for each person. The main thing is to believe that when you begin speaking, the Holy Spirit will give you inspired words to speak and they will likely be words or sounds that you don't understand. Speaking in tongues will seem strange at first, but rest assured, after just a little practice it will seem very normal to you. I'll give you two ideas that may help you get started.

1. Find someone who already speaks in tongues and ask them to pray with you to receive the gift. After or while praying, you may only speak a couple of "words" or phrases. Starting can be slow, but everyone's experience is unique so don't worry if words are not flowing quickly for you. Speak whatever comes to your mouth at the time. It's okay if you're not speaking sentences or paragraphs. Be patient. The more often you speak in tongues, the more the gift will flow.

2. Another way to start is to just pray by yourself for this gift. Believe that God will give this to you if you earnestly ask. Then open your mouth and begin to speak whatever comes out. It may be something that sounds merely like a few syllables, but again, the more you do this, the more easily the words and phrases will come through you. Sometimes you may feel that you are repeating just one phrase over and over again. Don't be concerned about that. Even in a standard prayer, we sometimes repeat phrases. For example, you might be praising God, saying, "Thank you Jesus, thank you Jesus" over and over. Just speak what comes and don't get your mind involved in trying to decipher it. Also, you may feel like you're "making it up." Many people worry about this in the beginning and they stop speaking in tongues and never get a chance to develop it fully. If you let your "intellect or logic" get in the way, you won't move forward easily—or you'll shut down the gift entirely. I would encourage you to set yourself free from thinking too much and understand that you are in a learning phase.

Notes

CHAPTER TWENTY-ONE

The Gift of Prophecy

WHEN GOD REVEALS SOMETHING FOR another person to you, and you speak what you hear to them, you're operating in what is known as the gift of prophecy. The gift of prophecy requires you to develop your ability to hear God's voice before it can function properly. God can give you messages for others, but if you aren't able to receive them, you can't give them to the people they're intended for. The gift of prophecy is not without controversy. One of the controversies is over the fact that what I just described sounds a bit like fortune telling.

Prophecy makes use of our ability to hear spiritual communication. Fortune telling also relies on a person's ability to hear spiritual communication. The difference between them is the source of the revelation. Prophecy is revelation which has its origin in God. Fortune tellers, psychics, and those who channel other spirits use the same mechanism to hear things that are said by spirits, but they are not God.

Because there is a bit of uncertainty about which spirit is behind any revelation, some have chosen to deny that the gift of prophecy is valid today. Once again, it comes down to a question of how much (or how little) risk you're willing to take. In spite of any risk, one of the most powerful uses of our ability to hear God's voice is the gift of prophecy. An accurate prophetic word, given at the right time, can bring hope to the despairing and reveal the destiny of someone who feels lost. The apostle Paul instructed the church at Corinth:

Pursue love, yet desire earnestly spiritual gifts, but especially that you may prophesy.
1 COR. 14:1 NASB

In Paul's mind, prophecy was one of the gifts we should desire most. He went on to explain that prophecy is not just for certain individuals, but for all believers. He also noted that the purpose for prophecy is to encourage others:

For you can all prophesy one by one, that all may learn and all may be encouraged.
1 COR. 14:31

When someone prophesies to us, we may learn things God wants us to know about our gifting, our relationships, our identity, our destiny, or other aspects of our life. We can learn about ourselves and about the plans God has for us.

God may reveal positive things about others to us, such as their gifting, talents, spheres of influence, and personal strengths. But He may also reveal negative things. One of the dangers of receiving revelation from God about others is that it may be used against them. God may disclose the dark secrets of a person's life to any of us. A person with a desire to tarnish another's reputation can easily use prophetic revelation to "correct" them simply to cause them shame or humiliation. Some believers have been brought before church elders for discipline based on things discerned about them by someone with a score to settle. Before we consider dragging someone's dirty laundry out in the open for public scrutiny, we might consider how we would feel if we were in the hot seat.

Prophetic revelation, if it is not used wisely, can cause church splits and destroy life-long friendships. It has as much potential to do harm as good, which is one reason why prophets have been removed from so many churches and the prophetic gifts of the Holy Spirit rejected. It may be that God will reveal the issues of sin that someone struggles with, but since prophecy is intended to *encourage* and not condemn, we must find a way to take the revelation we receive and speak it in a way that encourages. How do we accomplish this?

When God shows us a person's sin, He's revealing something about their character. What He reveals in this case is not how He intends for them to live, it is how they happen to be living at the moment. The goal of prophecy is not to expose that sin, but to inspire them to live as Jesus lived. The power of the prophecy is its ability to reveal the future. We have the responsibility of revealing the person they will become, and not the person they are today.

If for example, God speaks to you about a woman who has a problem with gossip, you must think about the damage that could be done if you confront her about it, publicly. Prophecy is not for the purpose of causing shame or humiliation. So it might be best to speak in terms of the great friend she *will* be and about how people *will* come to know her as a trusted and loyal friend. As hard as it might be to speak the opposite of what you know to be true at the present, God's goal for this woman is that she would be transformed. Prophecy declares and agrees with God's plans for our future. A prophetic word that reveals who God intends for her to be has the power to draw her into that destiny. And that is one of the goals of prophecy—to reveal who we are becoming.

God doesn't orchestrate our failures. He is the author of our faith and the one who brings our sanctification to completion. We all have in our spiritual DNA the blueprint for success, but most of us have never seen the blueprint. When we fail in some area, it is because we have allowed the enemy to lead us from the path God has prepared for us (see Jas. 1:13). Prophecy shines a light upon that path. Knowing that God has prepared a path and a destiny of righteousness for everyone, we must prophesy from the person's divinely ordained destiny, and not their failures. If God speaks about a man who is struggling with pornography, we may prophesy that he will live a life of purity.

When He reveals that a woman is struggling with addiction to alcohol, we have a choice: Do we reveal the addiction and warn them that it displeases God (as if they didn't already know) or do we declare God's desire for them to be a pillar of society and a role model for others? The first option will leave them feeling condemned and hopeless, while the second will leave them feeling encouraged.

Anyone who is reasonably observant can see the faults of others. It doesn't require revelation from the Spirit of God. But it does take the Spirit to reveal how He wants them to live. Prophecy always calls us to live in a place that is higher than where we're currently living. The prophetic word doesn't just call us higher—it carries the power of God to make the things we declare come to pass, if the hearer chooses to obey them. In the same way that there is a release of power when a spirit-filled believer prays for healing, there is a release of power when we prophesy according to the will of God. Since a prophetic word carries the power to bring to pass what we declare, if we declare a person to be a sinner, we're using the power of the Spirit to reinforce that identity. We must instead use the power of prophecy to establish their divine identity and destiny.

Giving a Prophetic Word

When I want to give someone a prophetic word, there are a couple of strategies I use. I usually begin by requesting information from God for them. This might sound obvious to some, but it's a step many of us may never consider. There's nothing wrong with asking God to give us specific revelation for an individual. Yes, He is God, but we're not being presumptuous or rude by asking Him to give us revelation for someone. The Bible says "we have not because we ask not." If you want to give someone a prophetic word, ask God to show you something specific about them. Here's a warning: Be prepared to receive something as soon as you ask. Many times the revelation God gives is nothing more than a brief thought impression, a word, or an image that flashes in our mind. It can appear quickly and then dissipate.

Soon after I began giving prophetic words, I was at a meeting when I received a word from a mature prophet. He looked at me and said,

"You doubt what God is saying. You're not sure that what you're hearing is from Him and here's what He wants you to know: The first thought that enters your mind after you've asked—that's Him." I've found this to be true. In most cases, the first thought impression that enters my mind after I've asked God for revelation is what He wants me to know.

After you've asked God to reveal something, expect Him to speak in whatever way He wants. It may be a thought impression. It might be an image in your mind or a series of images, or something that appears to be a video. It might be a strong emotion that suddenly grips you. It might be a sudden pain in your body. Try not to assume too much about what He's going to reveal to you.

After you've received the revelation, you might begin a dialog with Him to clarify what it means, if you're not certain. This can be particularly helpful if you're new to prophecy. You can have the conversation aloud as if you're talking to a friend nearby, or it can be in your mind between you and God. If you have questions, ask for clarification. You might receive new thought impressions, visions, or other revelation.

Once you're clear about what you want to say, simply say it to the person. You can use your normal tone of voice. It isn't necessary to raise your voice or to emphasize certain words. It isn't necessary to say things like "the Lord says" or "thus sayeth the Lord," or to call them "my son" or "my daughter." You don't need to be weird when you prophesy. I sometimes give people prophetic words in public places like hospitals. I can't afford to be dramatic or appear overly religious in these settings. It's fine to speak the way you would if you were having a normal conversation with a friend.

A few years ago, my wife and I visited a shopping mall while on vacation. As she looked for dresses, I gave people encouraging words. It began when I asked God for a word for a male store employee. In my mind's eye, I saw the word "insecurity," so I encouraged him in the area of developing strength and security in his life. I also asked God for a word for a female employee. As I closed my eyes, I saw the word "inspiration." I told her she was inspiring to others and that God would use her to be even more inspirational in the future. A prophetic word can be very short. It doesn't require you to get to know the people you're prophesying to, though if time allows, God can speak even more to them if you're able to spend a few minutes talking with them.

Be aware as you're giving a prophetic word of anything the Holy Spirit reveals to you that wasn't part of the initial message. You might speak for 30 seconds about the first impression you received, then you might receive a new impression. The new revelation can be about anything. If you began prophesying about their calling to heal the sick, God might suddenly show you something about their finances or marriage. The images you see and impressions you receive can flow like a river, so be ready to go with the flow. Many times the Holy Spirit will give me a single image, a single word, or a single thought to begin with. When I begin to prophesy from the initial image or impression, I receive two or three more impressions or images. Keep speaking what you receive until the flow of revelation ceases. Once the revelation has ceased, stop prophesying. Resist any temptation to add to what the Spirit has given you.

One day I picked up my daughter from High School and took her to the Department of Licensing to take her driving test. There was a man sitting behind me in the waiting room who had breathing problems. I could tell without looking at him by the sound he made as he breathed. I closed my eyes, asked the Holy Spirit for a word for him, and saw a beautiful purple background with drops of water falling from high above into a pond. I asked what it meant. I heard a thought impression in my mind which said, "These are my tears." I asked who the tears were for. I thought I knew, because my attention was on the man behind me. God confirmed this was a word for him. I got up and asked the man how he was doing. He said he was doing well. I told him about the vision and what it meant. I asked if I could pray for him, and he said, "I need all the prayer I can get." I prophesied and prayed a blessing over him.

Don't be afraid if you don't know the meaning or context of an image, a word, or an impression you receive. God will often give revelation that only has meaning to the one you're giving it to. For example, you might receive nothing except the number 102. The number will likely mean nothing to you, but you might tell the person you're prophesying to, "I'm not sure what it means, but I'm getting the number 102. Does that mean anything to you?" Wouldn't you be glad you took the risk and told them about the number when they reply, "How strange! I'm moving to a different apartment tomorrow. I was going to take an apartment downtown, because it's near where I work, but I was hoping one would come available in the suburbs. I checked with a landlord before I came here who said they have a nice apartment that just became available today. The number of the apartment is 102." Never underestimate God's ability to speak to our specific circumstances.

One day I transported a young woman with a tragic history. She suffered a dissecting aneurysm five years earlier, and had her aortic valve replaced due to valve failure. She suffered a stroke while she was in the hospital and lost her ability to speak. The stroke also caused right-side weakness. She had two children but she lived in a nursing home. She communicated by writing on a pad of paper. I asked God to show me things about her during the transport to the nursing home. I saw flowers and I got the impression that God wanted her to know she was more beautiful on the inside than any flower He ever created. I saw an image of a friend who is a gifted teacher. His image remained in my mind's eye for a long time. I believe it meant that she had a gift of teaching. In the background, I saw the word "healing." My partner and I took her to her room, then my partner left and went to the ambulance.

Our patient got off the gurney and went to put a blanket over her window to keep out the late afternoon sun. She fell while reaching up to put a tack in the wall to hold the blanket. I caught her as she fell. She began crying out of frustration. I gave her a hug and told her I'd put the blanket up. It was the perfect way for her to realize she could trust me. She went to her bed, sat down, and continued crying. I sat down next to her. "On the way here I asked God about you." I said. "He has a few things He wants you to know." She was eager to hear what I had to say.

"God wants you to know you're more beautiful inside than any flower He's ever made." We both began crying. It was hard for me to continue. She grabbed me and hugged me as tears streamed down her cheeks. I continued as more thought impressions came to mind, "God is pursuing you, and He's going to chase you every day for as long as it takes Him to win your heart. You have a gift of teaching and when you're ready, He wants you to teach others about His love. You can be healed, but you need to take your eyes off your present circumstances and look into the future which is full of hope." She continued crying as I spoke, then wiped her nose and hugged me again. It seemed as though she'd been waiting a long time for someone to bring her some good news. It was a divine meeting I'll never forget.

Accidental Prophecy

Another way to prophesy is when God suddenly and without warning adds His inspiration to your normal way of speaking. This might sound odd if you've never thought about it or experienced it, but the more aware you are of this phenomenon, the more you'll realize people do it all the time unknowingly.

Imagine you're having a conversation with a stranger while waiting to have the tires changed on your car. You're making small-talk and you feel an unusual connection to this stranger that seems odd. That ought to be the first clue that God is up to something. Unusually strong emotions we feel for strangers are often the means God uses to get us to deliver a message to them. You're talking to the stranger when she says she's been worried about her brother who is in the hospital with cancer. Without thinking, you blurt out that she doesn't need to worry about him. You reassure her that her brother is going to be fine, that the cancer will leave on its own, and that he'll be discharged from the hospital in a few days.

She thanks you for your words of encouragement, gets up, walks to the register, and pays her bill. As she leaves, she waves to you on the way out the door. Your mind is reeling, wondering why on earth you just told a complete stranger that her brother who has cancer would be fine. If anything like this has ever happened to you, there is a good chance you prophesied God's perspective of the situation to them and didn't even know it.

This happens to me from time to time in everyday conversations with friends. I'm engaged in a discussion when suddenly, I have knowledge of something I did not know a few minutes earlier, and could not possibly know unless God revealed it to me. When we're given a deep conviction or understanding of something we could not possibly know—it's likely we're receiving revelation from God. In the middle of the conversation we suddenly begin explaining the situation from God's perspective. We might encourage them or reassure them there's nothing to worry about. We might reveal some change in their circumstances they aren't aware of yet. Many times our knowledge isn't delivered as a prophetic word, but it is.

Exercise

The next time you're with a group of friends, ask if any of them would be willing to receive a prophetic word from you. If they agree, ask the Holy Spirit to show you something about them and deliver a prophetic word based on what He shows you. Ask if they sense that the revelation you gave them seemed to be from the heart of God. If they say no, don't get discouraged. It takes practice and persistence to develop the gift.

Notes

Notes

CHAPTER TWENTY-TWO

Three Gifts from God

IN THIS CHAPTER WE'LL DISCUSS three different, but related ways in which God speaks. These three are the spiritual gifts known as *the word of knowledge, the word of wisdom,* and *the discerning of spirits.* These gifts are often used in the context of healing and deliverance, though they have other applications as well. In order to better understand how they work, I'll provide a brief overview of the biblical model of healing which will illustrate why these gifts are necessary.

Jesus healed thousands of people of every disease imaginable and raised people from the dead, but confessed that His secret to success had to do with the *relationship* He had with His Father: "The Son does nothing, but what He sees the Father doing."

There are many people who advocate using a standard method to healing and deliverance. It's human nature to rely on a systematic approach that has worked in the past. Everything seems easier when we have a step-by-step process to follow. The problem is that although formulas can work, they don't always give us the results we're looking for. Many times it's only after our formula has failed that we resort to asking God how He wants to heal a person or set them free from a demon. What we ought to do is follow the example of Jesus.

Rather than using a standard approach, each time Jesus was confronted with someone who needed healing or deliverance, He sought the counsel of His Father to see what was needed in their case. His ministry was always directed by and in accordance with the will and knowledge of the Father.

I believe it is God's will to heal everyone. That's what Jesus revealed when He ministered to the sick. No one was turned away who needed healing. Everyone who requested it received it. Jesus is the best revelation of the will of God that we have and He revealed that it is the Father's will for all to be healed and set free of demonic oppression. I believe that any lack of healing we see today is due to the fact that we have not yet inquired of the Father about what is needed to set a particular person free.

God has chosen to release healing through believers like you and I. Jesus gave us all the authority we need to heal. The Holy Spirit, who lives in us, is the source of power for healing. We have access to everything we need, except in some cases, we lack the specific instructions from God about how a person should be healed. It's one thing to have power and authority for healing. It's another to understand how they are to be used.

Imagine for a moment a father who wants his sons to learn how to construct a building. He provides a level plot of land, the bricks, steel, concrete, electrical wiring, and all the other materials needed to construct the building. He also provides the heavy equipment and tools needed for the job. Now imagine his sons as they attempt to build a building without plans or instructions. The building site quickly turns into a mess. Everything they need is there, but without specific instructions about how to get the work done, the sons are doomed to failure. Healing and deliverance are designed to function in a similar way.

God has given us all that we need to operate effectively in healing and deliverance. We make a mess of it when we fail to go to Him for instruction and guidance as to how our power and authority are to be used. God doesn't make things difficult to discourage us. He allows us to face challenges and problems so that we would come to Him for the solutions. When we pray and a person is not healed or set free, what is missing is accurate information from the Father about what needs to be done.

The Word of Knowledge

God can reveal to us an almost unlimited number of things that can bring healing, or that will prevent it if we're unaware of them. Some of those things will be revealed to us by the Holy Spirit if we ask. The information can come to us in a number of ways. The word of knowledge is one of the gifts of the Holy Spirit mentioned in first Corinthians chapter 12. It is a way in which God imparts to us certain facts that we do not know. It is information about a situation that is true which is given to help bring His will to pass for that situation.

The gifts of the Holy Spirit may be easier to understand if we think of them as ways in which the Spirit of God "manifests" Himself to the world. To *manifest* something is to make it known. As God wishes to make Himself known to His creation, He manifests Himself through the spiritual gifts. Although the word of knowledge is a gift of the Spirit, it is a gift that can be given to any Spirit-filled believer at any time. It is not just for special individuals. If the Holy Spirit is in you, and if you are willing, He is able to manifest Himself through you in any way He chooses and at any time. Since one of the chief obstacles to healing and deliverance is our failure to recognize what is needed in each case, receiving words of knowledge can be extremely helpful, particularly for difficult cases. When we receive a word of knowledge it is as if we've been given a key to unlock a door.

Some people receive a word of knowledge through thought impressions they hear in their mind. Others receive them through dreams and visions. Some people receive them through the sudden onset of strong emotions. The emotion can be a clue to the emotion someone else is feeling, such as depression or hopelessness. Learning to receive words of knowledge comes by developing greater sensitivity to the leading of the Holy Spirit.

Once we receive a word of knowledge we must ask God what He wants us to do with it. A word of knowledge may be given to encourage us to pray for someone to be healed. One day while I was working on the ambulance, I wanted to pray for my patient, but I wasn't sure what conditions she had that needed prayer. I closed my eyes and in my mind's eye I saw the words "back pain," "insomnia," and "anxiety." I told my patient the things God showed me. She confirmed everything and allowed me to pray for her.

One Sunday morning my wife woke up with numbness in her hand and told me about it. I was curious, so I asked God why she had it. It seemed as though He said (I heard this as a thought impression in my mind) that it was a word of knowledge for healing. When we arrived at church that morning, I mentioned it to the pastor as a word of knowledge. Four people said they had been experiencing numbness in their hands and we prayed for all of them to be healed.

One day on the way home from work, I went to Starbucks for coffee. I placed my order and waited with other patrons. As I did, I closed my eyes and saw an image of the woman standing in front of me and the word "headaches." I also saw a name indicating that her name was Amanda. As I was leaving, I asked if her name was Amanda. She said, "Yes, how did you know?"

"God told me," I replied. "Do you have chronic headaches?"

"Yes, I do. Did God tell you about them?"

"As a matter of fact, He did. Can I pray with you to be healed?" She happily agreed.

One day I transported a woman in her late fifties who had terminal ovarian cancer. I asked God if she would be healed if I prayed for her and in my mind I heard the distinct word, "no." I asked why she would not be healed. I closed my eyes again and saw a heavenly vision of clouds with a beautiful mansion resembling a castle in its midst. I believe it represented the fact that she was soon going to be heaven-bound. I talked with her husband during the transport about what I saw. He was very grateful. He took it as confirmation that she would soon be in paradise and her suffering would be over.

The Word of Wisdom

The word of wisdom is another gift (or manifestation) of the Holy Spirit that is mentioned in first Corinthians chapter 12. The word of wisdom is similar to the word of knowledge. It is wisdom about a situation that we would not normally have. The difference between a word of knowledge and a word of wisdom can be seen when we understand the difference between knowledge and wisdom. Knowledge is information about something in particular. It is the facts we must know about an issue. Wisdom is knowing what should be done with the information we have or the action we should take once we know the facts. Wisdom is knowledge correctly applied. In some cases a word of wisdom will instruct you about what actions you ought to take.

Before I go into a job interview, I usually ask God for any revelation He wants to give me about the interview process and I spend a few minutes in silence waiting for His reply. I sometimes receive images in my mind concerning things I've said in past job interviews that I might mention. Sometimes I'll receive images of calls I've responded to in the past. Sometimes I'll see flashes of conversations I've had with coworkers. Since God knows the mind of the interviewer and what they might be looking for in a candidate, I take these impressions as suggestions about things I should be ready to discuss in the interview.

Sometimes a word of wisdom will instruct you about something you should not do. One day my partner and I transported an elderly man who fell at home. Based on his symptoms, it seemed as though he might have had a hip fracture. We placed him on a plastic backboard to make it easier to lift him onto the gurney. My partner asked if I was going to start an IV and give him morphine. I observed our patient and noticed that as long as we didn't move him too much he seemed to be tolerating the pain pretty well. I received a thought impression in my mind which seemed like a message from God that said, "He doesn't need morphine." To be honest, I wasn't certain it was God. But I proceeded as if it was, and we transported the man without giving him morphine. During the transport his pain gradually subsided. By the time we got him to the hospital the pain was almost gone. Having seen people healed in the ambulance before without prayer, I wondered if it was another case of the Holy Spirit healing someone by simply manifesting His presence. It's difficult to explain how placing him on a hard plastic board and driving him over bumpy roads would make him feel better. I believe I received a word of wisdom telling me He would be healed if we simply transported him and allowed God to do the healing during the trip.

Words of wisdom can be given for just about any kind of situation. My family has a tradition of gathering in snowy locations over the Christmas holidays. One year it was decided the family would be gathering in New York. From the moment I first heard of the plan, I had a sense that something would foul things up. When my family asked if I was going to be there, I politely declined. When they asked why, I explained that I had a feeling as though the weather was going to cause problems. Not understanding how God forewarns us about these things, they were disappointed. But I stuck by my convictions and stayed home. That Christmas, New York City received almost two feet of snow and experienced extremely gusty winds. Most of the main streets were impassable for days. All the airports in the area were closed and inbound flights were diverted to other cities. Many outbound flights were canceled. Some of my brothers and sisters had to take extra time off work because they could not get flights back home until the mess from the snowstorm had been cleaned up.

I believe I had received a word of wisdom about my plans. I didn't just receive information about an approaching storm. God told me what plans to make in order to avoid having travel problems.

After I had published the first two books in this series, God began giving me dreams suggesting that I consider mentoring other authors. One night I had a dream about one author in particular who was in the process of writing an excellent book. He became discouraged and considered giving up on the book completely. From my perspective in the dream, I could see that the enemy was not happy about the potential impact the book would have, so an effort was organized by the enemy to discourage him and prevent the book from being published. In the dream, I knew my part was to encourage the author and help him see the book through to completion. Right now I'm the administrator of an online group of more than 200 writers. I'm personally mentoring some of the authors God has shown me in dreams. This is another case where God didn't just give me information about someone, but specific actions I should take in order to help them.

As I've become more involved in emotional healing, I've had a number of instructive dreams. In one dream I was interviewing mental health patients to determine if I could legally treat them. During the interviews, I realized I could not legally treat some of them under the current definition I was using, so I rewrote the definition and broadened it. This allowed me to treat more people. The point of this dream was that there are many more people who need healing than I first suspected and that I needed to think in broader terms. This dream is typical of how God makes me aware of problems with how I'm operating. The adjustments I need to make are illustrated in the dreams.

The Discerning of Spirits

The discerning of spirits is another gift of the Holy Spirit mentioned in First Corinthians chapter 12. As with all the other gifts, it is a way in which the Holy Spirit manifests Himself to us. It is available to any believer. The way in which this gift operates in us will be determined by how well we've developed our spiritual senses and how well we've become acquainted with sensing the different ways in which God speaks.

Although this gift can be used to discern the presence and character of evil spirits, it can also be used to detect heavenly spirits. When this gift is in operation, we might be able to discern the specific nature of demons that we would not otherwise know. We might be given the names or areas of specialization of the evil spirits. Some demons specialize in creating feelings of despair or hopelessness, while others may tempt us with sexual sin. Some specialize in creating attitudes of religious superiority or self-importance. Heavenly spirits also specialize, but in positive ways. Some angels bring messages, some are responsible for healing, and others bring spiritual revival. Sometimes the area of specialization of a spirit is revealed by its name.

Some people are able to smell the presence of evil spirits as an odor like rotten eggs or sulfur. Some detect the presence of angels by the presence of the scent of flowers or one of many different sweet or savory aromas. It might seem as if we smell these odors with our physical sense of smell, but it is our spiritual sense of smell that is at work.

Many people see demons and angels as they are revealed by the Holy Spirit. Sometimes they are seen with the eyes open. Sometimes they're seen with the eyes closed. They can appear either as a vision in our mind or as a scene that is external to us. It doesn't matter how we sense a spirit's presence. The revelation of any spirit, regardless of how it is done, has the same purpose. Spirits are usually (though not always) revealed so that we might interact with them for a specific purpose. That purpose can be discovered by asking the Holy Spirit. There will be occasions when the revealing of a spirit is simply to make us aware that it is there without a need to interact with it.

Healing can be done more effectively as we become more aware of how angels are involved in the process. Many people I've interviewed have testified of seeing angels of healing at work—usually at meetings and conferences that are held for the specific purpose of healing and deliverance. If you have not seen healing personally, and if you wonder if it is a legitimate phenomenon, you might consider attending one of these healing meetings to see for yourself. In such meetings, angels are often discerned as they carry containers of oil, that when poured over the sick, bring healing.

Angels of healing operate in many different ways. I heard a testimony from a man who sees angels during healing conferences quite often. At one conference he was praying for a man who needed healing of a brain tumor. As he prayed he saw an angel holding what looked like a torch. The angel held the torch to the man's head with the flame aimed at the part of his brain where the tumor was located. After the prayer session, the man reported feeling a very strong sensation of heat inside his head. He later reported that he had been healed as a result of this encounter.

Exercise

The next time you are around a group of people, quiet your soul and ask the Holy Spirit to give you some revelation about another person's need. Ask for specific details. Ask the Holy Spirit to clarify anything that isn't clear to you. Share the information with the person it pertains to and ask if you can pray for them.

Notes

Notes

CHAPTER TWENTY-THREE

The Greatest of These

WE'VE LOOKED AT THE GIFTS of the Spirit and how Paul taught the church in Corinth their proper use. The believers in Corinth were incredibly gifted. They spoke with the tongues of angels, heard the voice of God accurately, and knew how to heal the sick. When comparing his letters to ones he wrote to other churches, it's apparent that they were head and shoulders above the rest with regard to spiritual gifts. Such proficiency might lead us to think they'd reached the pinnacle of spiritual life. We might think that operating in the gifts of the Spirit makes us spiritually mature, but this is not the case.

The believers in Corinth were *both* the most spiritually gifted, but the most spiritually immature of all the early churches. Much of what Paul had to say in other parts of his letter were corrective words that addressed their immature attitudes toward one another. He reminded them that spiritual maturity is not a matter of operating proficiently in spiritual gifts, but of becoming a person who consistently shows love to others:

> *"Though I speak with the tongues of men and of angels, but have not love, I have become sounding brass or a clanging cymbal. And though I have the gift of prophecy, and understand all mysteries and all knowledge, and though I have all faith, so that I could remove mountains, but have not love, I am nothing. And though I bestow all my goods to feed the poor, and though I give my body to be burned, but have not love, it profits me nothing."*
> 1 COR 13:1-3

There are many who would like to operate more proficiently in the spiritual gifts, but the gifts are not an end in themselves. We can seek them for the wrong reasons. They don't demonstrate that we've achieved something great. They're intended to be a manifestation of God's love. The reasons why we seek the gifts can sometimes reveal a wrong sense of identity. Allow me to illustrate this point:

There were many Jewish leaders who opposed the ministry of Jesus. The scribes and Pharisees were often mentioned in the gospels as being antagonistic to Him. The scribes and Pharisees were seen as religious experts. People held them in high esteem because of their knowledge of the scriptures. But Jesus drew people away from them. When the crowds showed preference to Him, the scribes and Pharisees became envious and plotted to kill Him.

These leaders were motivated to be seen as experts because it gave them a sense of significance. No child ever dreams of growing up to be insignificant. We're born with a desire to do great things. Our true significance is given to us by God, who created each of us with a divine purpose in mind. Once we understand what that purpose is and accept it, it begins to manifest in all that we do. The scribes and Pharisees didn't understand that they were God's beloved children. They saw themselves as orphans. They didn't know that He had planned great things for them, so they sought greatness on their own.

When you see yourself as an orphan, you believe it's up to you to make the best life for yourself. Many Christians, who profess that God is their

Father, live from the belief that He has little interest in taking care of them or helping them find their destiny. They see Him doing these things for others, but not for them. They secretly believe He must have favorites and that they are not among the favored few. When you don't understand who you truly are, you'll strive to become someone that you are not. You attempt to find significance on your own. Orphans seek to have their need for significance met by the world. And the world cannot do that which God intends to do Himself.

The child of God must allow their needs to be met by Him. Having our needs met by Him removes the expectation that we must have them met by the world. This allows us the freedom to love others without conditions and without expecting anything in return. If the world doesn't treat us the way we expect, it doesn't matter. We can rest in the knowledge that the God who created all things loves us.

We cannot love God until we first know that He loves us. The knowledge that He loves us transforms our heart into one that has the capacity to love Him back. Neither can we love other humans before we apprehend His love for us. His love changes our heart and makes it capable of loving those who seem to us to be unlovable. Once we know how loved we are by God, we can show that same love to others. God is love and we are intended to be His expression of love to the world. If you take nothing else away from this book, let it be the simple fact that you are greatly loved by Him and that He desires to meet all your needs, so that you can live out your unique destiny and express His love in the way that only *you* can.

THANK YOU FOR PURCHASING THIS BOOK

For inspiring articles and an up-to-date list of my books,
go to my website, **PrayingMedic.com**.

Other books by **Praying Medic**

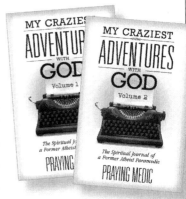

Divine Healing
Made Simple

Seeing in the Spirit
Made Simple

My Craziest Adventures with God
Volumes 1 and 2

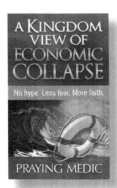

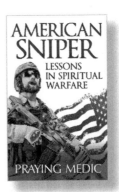

A Kingdom View of
Economic Collapse

American Sniper:
Lessons in Spiritual Warfare

Emotional Healing
in 3 Easy Steps

FUTURE BOOKS

I HAVE AN ENTIRE SERIES of books planned to help train and equip the saints for the work of ministry. Here are the titles of future books in the series, *The Kingdom of God Made Simple:*

Power & Authority Made Simple

Deliverance & Inner Healing Made Simple

Traveling in the Spirit Made Simple

Made in the USA
Middletown, DE
03 June 2018